Critical Pedagogy

Languages for Intercultural Communication and Education
Editors: Michael Byram, *University of Durham, UK*
Alison Phipps, *University of Glasgow, UK*

The overall aim of this series is to publish books which will ultimately inform learning and teaching, but whose primary focus is on the analysis of intercultural relationships, whether in textual form or in people's experience. There will also be books which deal directly with pedagogy, with the relationships between language learning and cultural learning, between processes inside the classroom and beyond. They will all have in common a concern with the relationship between language and culture, and the development of intercultural communicative competence.

Other Books in the Series
Audible Difference: ESL and Social Identity in Schools
    Jennifer Miller
Context and Culture in Language Teaching and Learning
    Michael Byram and Peter Grundy (eds)
Critical Citizens for an Intercultural World: Foreign Language Education as Cultural Politics
    Manuela Guilherme
Developing Intercultural Competence in Practice
    Michael Byram, Adam Nichols and David Stevens (eds)
How Different Are We? Spoken Discourse in Intercultural Communication
    Helen Fitzgerald
An Intercultural Approach to English language Teaching
    John Corbett
Intercultural Experience and Education
    Geof Alred, Michael Byram and Mike Fleming (eds)

Other Books of Interest
Age and the Acquisition of English as a Foreign Language
    María del Pilar García Mayo and Maria Luisa García Lecumberri (eds)
Age, Accent and Experience in Second Language Acquisition
    Alene Moyer
Effects of Second Language on the First
    Vivian Cook (ed.)
Foreign Language and Culture Learning from a Dialogic Perspective
    Carol Morgan and Albane Cain
The Good Language Learner
    N. Naiman, M. Fröhlich, H.H. Stern and A. Todesco
Language, Culture and Communication in Contemporary Europe
    Charlotte Hoffman (ed.)
Language Learners as Ethnographers
    Celia Roberts, Michael Byram, Ana Barro, Shirley Jordan and Brian Street
Language Teachers, Politics and Cultures
    Michael Byram and Karen Risager
Motivating Language Learners
    Gary N. Chambers
New Perspectives on Teaching and Learning Modern Languages
    Simon Green (ed.)
Teaching and Assessing Intercultural Communicative Competence
    Michael Byram

Please contact us for the latest book information:
Multilingual Matters , Frankfurt Lodge, Clevedon Hall,
Victoria Road, Clevedon, BS21 7HH, England
http://www.multilingual-matters.com

LANGUAGES FOR INTERCULTURAL
COMMUNICATION AND EDUCATION 8
Series Editors: Michael Byram and Alison Phipps

Critical Pedagogy
Political Approaches to Language and Intercultural Communication

Edited by
Alison Phipps and Manuela Guilherme

MULTILINGUAL MATTERS LTD
Clevedon • Buffalo • Toronto • Sydney

Library of Congress Cataloging in Publication Data
Critical Pedagogy: Political Approaches to Language and Intercultural Communication
Edited by Alison Phipps and Manuela Guilherme
Languages for Intercultural Communication and Education: 8
Includes bibliographical references.
1. Language and languages – Study and teaching. 2. Multicultural education.
I. Phipps, Alison M. II. Guilherme, Manuela. III. Series.
P53.45.C75 2004
418'.007–dc22   2003025671

British Library Cataloguing in Publication Data
A catalogue entry for this book is available from the British Library.

ISBN 1-85359-753-8 (hbk)

Multilingual Matters Ltd
UK: Frankfurt Lodge, Clevedon Hall, Victoria Road, Clevedon BS21 7HH.
USA: UTP, 2250 Military Road, Tonawanda, NY 14150, USA.
Canada: UTP, 5201 Dufferin Street, North York, Ontario M3H 5T8, Canada.
Australia: Footprint Books, PO Box 418, Church Point, NSW 2103, Australia.

Printed and bound in Great Britain by Biddles Ltd.

Contents

Introduction: Why Languages and Intercultural Communication Are Never Just Neutral[1]

As academics, we are engaged, in various ways, in a project to teach others and to be taught, to enable learning and to learn ourselves. We daily live out the challenge of how to *be* with the complex knowledges we have or seek, that we can enable fresh perspectives, new criticisms, new ways of being that may be resources for hope.

Our subject in this book is that of Critical Pedagogy, examined in the context of a broader project to engage with questions of language(s) and intercultural communication. It is not, perhaps, a topic that presents itself as immediately linked to the concerns that focus on the relationship between language, languages and intercultural communication. Critical pedagogy is, after all, a well-established field with its own key names, principles, limits and its own ways of proceeding. Language and Intercultural Communication is much more a field in formation, searching and exploring thematic concerns and potential edges, looking for inspiration from further afield as well as growing its own ideas.

From the start, the journal *Language and Intercultural Communication*, edited by Alice Tomic and Crispin Thurlow, has developed in partnership with the *International Association for Languages and Intercultural* (IALIC). Their invitation to develop a special issue of the journal led also to this edited volume. Work aimed at examining the relationship between questions of language and intercultural communication does not necessarily seek out scholars wishing to present on themes relating to pedagogy, but education has been a formative ground for our endeavours. Language(s) and intercultural communication are seen as a challenging component of teaching experiences. Many of those whose work has been manifestly influential in growing the field of language and intercultural communication have come from the field of education. Michael Byram, Genevieve Zarate, Claire Kramsch, Henri Giroux, Ronald Barnett are but a few of the names that have come to circulate in our common discussions of languages and intercultural communication (Barnett, 1994, 1997, 2000; Byram & Fleming, 1998; Byram, 1997; Byram, Nichols & Stevens, 2001; Byram, Zarate & Neuner, 1997; Giroux, 1988, 1992; Kramsch, 1993).

But why not just pedagogy? Why critical pedagogy? Critical pedagogy means addressing radical concerns, the abuses of power in intercultural contexts, in the acquisition of languages and in their circulation. And this work is never just neutral. As intellectuals, scholars and educators, the editors, the readers and the contributors to this book are engaged in, among other things, the critical tradition of cultural studies and of longer Marxian critique, in examining and challenging common sense assumptions, hegemonic structures and any uncritical belief in the status quo. This work is in a field where social experiences are in solution, where there is very little that can actually be said with any degree of certainty. Indeed, we all of us live in worlds which are 'supercomplex' (Barnett,

2000), not just complex; these worlds require our active engagement and our creative practice as intellectuals. This creativity and energy cannot come without the foundations of disciplined, determined, critical work.

Work in this book is clearly committed both to the struggle and grief of criticism, of a stance towards the world that takes on the world and its problems and inequalities. It also publicly and determinedly articulates the problems that persist in accepting the world as it now is. It refuses to place faith in the status quo of relations forged only in the dominant interests of global capitalism, of white hegemonic power, of world English as a supreme or first language, of a so-called 'first world', of patriarchal power and of heterosexuality.

It is our firm conviction that the project of pedagogy in languages and intercultural communication is not a cynical functionalist project that manufactures intercultural and linguistic competences like biscuits, and creates docile bodies fit to serve a machine of global capitalism. No. It is our conviction that pedagogy is an unpredictable business, but a business which is about hope, politics, power and practicality.

Those of us in the field of language and intercultural communication are constantly in situations where we are negotiating power, watching it shift and play between all our encounters as we use words from different languages, as we *language* in our own tongue and we attempt, in often broken, yet always profoundly hopeful ways, to reach out to others, and to communicate. Indeed, following Derrida (Derrida, 1976), and Young (Young, 1996), we know that our work with words, any words, has to be based not in the facticity of meanings expressed as words, but in the hope that we can use language in the belief and trust that, for all its attendant complex difficulties, meaning may indeed be made. We have to live as if this is true, particularly in our pedagogic contexts.

With Giroux we acknowledge that this is a volatile business, placing teachers in the position of carrying knowledges in themselves, opening their bodies out to what are still largely young people, despite many access programmes and initiatives for long learning or continuing education. We have the daunting challenge, in our intercultural communicative contexts, of engaging the bodies of the young, for the project of living with supercomplexity as critical beings.

This strand of pedagogy is one chosen out of intellectual, ethical and practical conviction. It provides a way for those of us engaging with the concerns of language and intercultural communication to approach our practice as teachers critically and pedagogically. It gives us a way of being imaginative voices from the margins and from the edge. Critical Pedagogy requires that we detach ourselves from the order of things as they are and that we speak critically unto power. It requires refusing the language of the dominant, the functionalist, the positivist; the ways of essentialising and of simply making our own practice serve the goal of implementing things in ways which serve the smooth running of a safe system, but which never enable change or the questioning of power.

Critical Pedagogy is a human way of being in the world that does not seek to live simply or painlessly with conditions of affluence and plenty for some and not for all. It is a way of *doing being critical* and doing pedagogy, a way of engaging primarily, though not entirely, with the marginal and the burdened among us – namely, following Giroux's piece in this volume, the young and all those who come to us vulnerable and open and ready to learn.

Critical Pedagogy never arrives, it continually takes us beyond our own boundaries and beyond ourselves and into realms of respect for those very boundaries and ways of being of others. But it does not uncritically respect the boundaries of power that tell us how the world should be or how we should do our educating. It refuses to entertain regimes of education that operate to serve values of employability, continued 'progress' and growth in the markets, and the so-called 'knowledge economy'. It refuses to simply allow colonising moves or the commodification of knowledge and of the bodies of the young to pass without comment.

A critical pedagogy of (foreign) language/culture education and of intercultural communication/interaction implies a critical use of language(s), a critical approach to one's own and other cultural backgrounds and a critical view of intercultural interaction. As proposed by Paulo Freire and as developed by Moacir Gadotti (Director of the Instituto Paulo Freire in São Paulo, Brasil), Henry Giroux and other authors such as Peter McLaren, Carlos Alberto Torres, Barry Kanpol, Joan Wink, and so on, Critical Pedagogy offers important guidelines for the study of language(s) and intercultural communication. Amongst the concepts proposed and elaborated by the above-mentioned authors, as Guest Editors we would like to highlight here some that we believe contain the richest potential for language/culture educators, namely, reflection, dissent, difference, dialogue, empowerment, action and hope.

The importance of **reflection** in education is unquestionable, however, this strategy has been too often neglected in the study of culture and cultural difference as well as in the development of intercultural awareness; it has been replaced by the memorisation and interpretation of facts and by cultural generalisations or even stereotyping. Despite the fact that other leading pedagogues had previously emphasised this pedagogical strategy, John Dewey for example (although this was also one of the ideas he put forward that was most neglected by his followers), Critical Pedagogy has put a special focus on reflection, not necessarily analysis, geared to cultural and political awareness.

Critical reflection can therefore be considered a fundamental strategy for the development of critical cultural awareness and of a critical understanding of intercultural interaction. In this volume Diaz-Greenberg and Nevin, for example, underline the importance of critical reflection for student teachers as a means by which they may become more aware of the implications of their personal and professional experiences and of their role as critical pedagogues.

Dissent is another element that has been put forward by critical pedagogues and which may change the perspective towards intercultural interaction since the latter has often erroneously established intercultural consensus and harmony as its only goal. Competencies for intercultural interaction entail the capacity to deal critically and successfully with dissent and even conflict through critical cultural awareness towards the Self and the Other and through honest and balanced negotiation.

Additionally, the notion of **difference** is intrinsic to the world of multiculturalism and interculturality. Henry Giroux introduced an important dimension, that is cultural, social and political, to Critical Pedagogy through the notion of a 'border pedagogy'. This idea is fundamental for a critical pedagogy of, for example, foreign language/culture education and of intercultural interaction in that it re-defines its nature, its content and its process. It rejects its traditional elitism and reliance on linguistic and cultural canons and standards, by allowing in difference and by breaking down social barriers and preconceived notions about the 'inferior' or 'superior' Other. Diaz-Greenberg and Nevin, again, illustrate such procedures by calling for more focus on emerging *proficiency* rather than on *deficiencies*.

Dialogue is another fundamental element for Critical Pedagogy that obviously brings in enormous potential for language and intercultural communication. However, critical dialogue is not idle chitchat since it is linked with critical reflection and critical action. This is probably the most controversial element among critical pedagogues when they attempt to go deeper into its theorisation and specification as it becomes evident later in this volume with the discussion about the constitutive nature of communication within a critical pedagogy by Warren *et al.*

In fact, critical dialogue, considered as the nexus between critical reflection and critical action, embodies the *praxis* of a *corpus* of knowledge/performance composed by critical cultural awareness and critical intercultural communication/interaction, which is of utmost importance in the theory and practice of language/culture education. The concept of **empowerment** is intertwined in the elements mentioned above but deserves, however, to be singled out in the description of a critical pedagogy and, in particular, of a critical pedagogy of language/culture education.

The empowerment of both teachers and students happens through the practice of critical reflection and critical dialogue and the recognition of difference and dissent and is expressed through the validation of their voices. In this volume, for example, Giroux is very clear about the need to give voice to the sufferings of the children and of the young people in this world; those who are submitted to sexual abuse, to starvation, to warfare, to racism, to the demands of the economic markets, to educational systems that do not prepare them to be critical citizens in this world; systems that neither allow or require them to make the most of their present lives both as individuals and as members of communities. Giroux summarises this need here by calling for a 'pedagogy of responsibility' that educates young people simultaneously for a professional future and for critical citizenship.

A pedagogy of responsibility is an essential element for citizenship education and, in the way Giroux puts it, it is not restricted to the teachers'/students' immediate context. Therefore, a pedagogy of responsibility is a relevant dimension to be included in the teaching about language and intercultural communication in that it establishes a link between the latter and citizenship education from a local/global perspective. Turner, in her chapter, exemplifies these struggles when she shows the struggles inherent in serving the dual goals of linguistic clarity and of creative empowerment for a postgraduate student. In this case, the teaching of foreign languages too often take Self and Other, viewed as independent and closed entities, as the basis for the construction of intercultural knowledge and exchange.

A pedagogy of responsibility, in Giroux's terms, thereby promotes an interdisciplinary approach and intercultural interaction on a critical basis within a global/local scope and is, therefore, enlightening for the study of cultural difference and for the definition of intercultural awareness. Finally, the achievement of empowerment sets the stage for the last, but not least, of the concepts, mentioned above, that are indispensable for a critical pedagogy, namely **action** and **hope**.

Both elements are essential for a transformative pedagogy, that is, for a pedagogy of responsibility for the world and for the people around us, in a closer and in a wider context. Students/teachers cannot of course take responsibility for everything, for that would mean take responsibility for nothing, but they can instead establish targets according to certain criteria and objectives. Language/culture educators will certainly find within their syllabus targets for action and motives for hopeful commitments across languages/cultures. The role of language/culture educators will necessarily be re-constructed so that it can meet the model of a 'public worker' and a 'cultural worker' as proposed, respectively, by Giroux and Freire.

Reflection, dissent, difference, dialogue, empowerment, action and hope all look towards renewal. For new worlds and new energy to come into the world several things are necessary. These are not things that can be learned and applied, they rise up out of different circumstances of poverty and plenty and they take different forms according to the paradoxes and supercomplexities of every circumstance that is to be challenged. According to Brueggemann (Brueggemann, 2000) renewal begins with lament. Newness can only come once the pain and the grief, so long held in and managed and declared invisible, so long numbed into normality, are publicly expressed.

Here, in this volume, are the heartfelt, rigorously researched, dissenting articulation of grief and anger. This is grief and publicly expressed pain that comes from the scholarly work of lingering over the questions and contexts that being a critical pedagogue requires. It is a pain expressed on behalf of the world's youth and of the youth of the Americas, of the children who are killed in conflict and as a result of conflict and who do not have anyone to speak for them – or precious few.

And in Giroux's generous and typically courageous public expression of pain we are challenged, through the work of Bourdieu, to end our complacency and engage as public intellectuals in the struggles for spaces for the young. We are challenged to stop the dominant forms of intercultural communication being in the form of a bomb down Baghdad high street, another manifest engagement with the other when another child has her limb blasted apart and away for ever as a result of our desire to communicate our power and our values of freedom to others. Here is an angry grief, fully controlled and held steady by the work of scholarly reflection and critical necessity.

Those of us associated with this critical project of language(s) and intercultural communication wish to offer resources for imagination, empowerment and hope. We find concepts and ideas of communication can be sifted and made anew, often controversially, providing us with ways of engaging with the world that shift our focus and make us more able to take bolder steps in our thinking and in our pedagogy. We find new voices brought, dialogically, into our debates about intercultural communication that give us a different vantage point, that can refresh perspectives that tire only too quickly when power is slick and the tedium we are constantly subject to, for the sake of bureaucratic unimaginings, threatens to suck up all our life and time, space and will to engage.

Critical Pedagogy was born in the circumstances of oppression, not of well being . In the field of language and intercultural communication we have stories to tell that are critical, resourceful, hopeful and also stories to tell that are of grief, of frustration, dissent and of Critical Pedagogy thwarted. It may be that we can pretend that the articulation of pain and the resources for hope do not belong in our pedagogy, that pedagogy should be neutral and that languages, intercultural communication and teaching, far from being political, are merely servants of the smooth running of global capitalism. But that would mean that our project in this journal becomes one of 'illiteracy' in the language of hope and a practising of a language that numbs and masks. And that fails us in our aim to promote work that resists reductive and hegemonic interpretations and that, instead, may contribute to understanding, dialogue and co-operation.

Editors: Manuela Guilherme and Alison Phipps
LAIC Editors: Alice Tomic and Crispin Thurlow

Note

1. We are indebted to Alice Tomic and Crispin Thurlow for agreeing to our proposal to edit a special issue of their journal *Language and Intercultural Communication*, on the theme of Critical pedagogy. Without their encouragement and scholarly insight, this particular volume would never have come in to being.

References

Barnett, R. (1994) *The Limits of Competence: Knowledge, Higher Education and Society.* Buckingham: Open University Press.
Barnett, R. (1997) *Higher Education: A Critical Business.* Buckingham: Open University Press.
Barnett, R. (2000) *Realizing the University in an Age of Supercomplexity.* Buckingham: Open University Press.
Brueggemann, W. (2000) *Texts that Linger, Words that Explode. Minneapolis:* Augsburg-Fortress.
Byram, M. (1997) *Teaching and Assessing Intercultural Communicative Competence.* Clevedon: Multilingual Matters.
Byram, M. and Fleming, M. (1998) *Language Learning in Intercultural Perspective: Approaches Through Drama and Ethnography.* Cambridge: Cambridge University Press.
Byram, M., Nichols, A. and Stevens, D. (2001) *Developing Intercultural Communication in Practice.* Clevedon: Multilingual Matters.
Byram, M., Zarate, G. and Neuner, G. (1997) *Sociocultural Competence in Language Learning and Teaching.* Strasbourg: Council of Europe Publishing.
Derrida, J. (1976) *Of Grammatology.* London: Johns Hopkins Press.
Freire, P. (1998) *Teachers as Cultural Workers.* Boulder, CO: Westview Press.
Giroux, H. (1988) *Teachers as Intellectuals.* New York: Bergin & Garvey.
Giroux, H. (1992) *Border Crossings: Cultural Workers and the Politics of Education.* London: Routledge.
Kramsch, C. (1993) *Context and Culture in Language Teaching.* Oxford: Oxford University Press
Okri, B. (1997) *A Way of Being Free.* London: Phoenix House.
Young, R. (1996) *Intercultural Communication: Pragmatics, Genealogy, Deconstruction.* Clevedon: Multilingual-Matters.

1 Betraying the Intellectual Tradition: Public Intellectuals and the Crisis of Youth

Henry A. Giroux
Penn State University, Pennsylvania, USA

Building upon the late Pierre Bourdieu's belief that intellectuals had a major responsibility in bridging intellectual work and the operation of politics, this paper argues that intellectuals, especially those in higher education, need to recognise that youth is an important moral referent and political starting point for addressing a number of issues related to a wide ranging number of political problems, including environmental and class concerns to matters of race, gender, and disability. Youth invokes compassion and understanding, which are crucial to shaping the civic imagination. The emphasis on young people's experience is important because it foregrounds the relationship between power and the lived realities shaped by material relations of power. More specifically, young people provide a more crucial lens through which hegemony can be analysed, compassion mobilised, and politics engaged beyond local interests and national boundaries. Educators need a new language in which young people are not detached from politics but become central to any transformative notion of pedagogy conceived in terms of social and public responsibility.

El fallecido Pierre Bourdieu estaba convencido de que era responsabilidad de los intelectuales construir puentes entre el trabajo intelectual y la política como actividad. En esta ponencia se plantea la obligación de los intelectuales, sobre todo los que trabajan en la educación terciaria, de reconocer que la juventud es un referente moral y un punto de partida político para enfrentar una gama de cuestiones y problemas políticos, entre ellos temas de ecología y de clase, tanto como de etnia, de género y de discapacidad. La juventud despierta la compasión y la comprensión, elementos imprescindibles en el despertar de la imaginación cívica. Es importante hacer hincapié en las experiencias de los jóvenes porque colocan en primera plana la relación entre el poder y las vivencias conformadas por las relaciones materiales de poder. Para precisar; los jóvenes nos dan una lente clave a través de la cual analizar la hegemonía, movilizar la compasión y comprometerse con una política que va más allá de los intereses locales y las fronteras nacionales. Los pedagogos necesitan un lenguaje nuevo que lejos de desvincular a los jóvenes de la política los ubique en el centro de toda noción transformadora de la pedagogia, concebida en un marco de responsabilidad social y política.

Keywords: culture, youth, critical pedagogy, public intellectuals, education

> The question that I would like to raise is this: Can intellectuals, and especially scholars, intervene in the political sphere? Must intellectuals partake in political debates as such, and if so, under what conditions can they interject themselves efficiently? What role can researchers play in the various social movements, at the national level and especially at the international level–that is, at the level where the fate of individuals and societies is increasingly being decided today? Can intellectuals contribute to inventing a new manner of doing politics fit for the novel dilemmas and threats of our age? (Bourdieu, 2000: 40)

Pierre Bourdieu was deeply concerned about the role that intellectuals might play as a progressive force for entering into the realm of politics. He believed that academics were indispensable, given their rigorous competencies as researchers, writers, and teachers, to creating the pedagogical conditions that both furthered social and economic justice and challenged the forms of symbolic and material domination that was being exercised globally, especially under the control of neoliberalism. Rejecting the commonplace assumption that academic work should be separate from the operations of politics, he reclaimed the role of the intellectual as an engaged social agent and 'maintained that intellectuals have a fearsome form of social responsibility' (Stabile & Morooka, 2003: 326). Following Edward Said, Noam Chomsky and others, Bourdieu was clear that for academics to become public intellectuals they had to betray the legacy of professionalism and specialism that has often positioned educators as narrow specialists, unencumbered by matters of ethics, power, and ideology, and wedded to a kind of sterile objectivity which justifies a wide variety of forms of escapism. Against the notion of professionalism, Bourdieu posits the notion of committed intellectuals in search of realist utopias.

But committed scholarship, for Bourdieu, does not mean limiting politics, pedagogy, or social change to the world of text or the narrow province of discourse. Nor does committed scholarship and pedagogy provide an excuse for those intellectuals who often 'mistake revolutions of the order of words, or texts, for revolutions in the order of things, to mistake verbal sparring at academic conferences for interventions in the affairs of [public life]' (Bourdieu, 2001: 41). According to Bourdieu, academics had not only to engage in a permanent critique of the abuses of authority in the larger social world, but also address the deadening scholasticism that often characterised work in the academy. This was not simply a call for them to renounce an all too common form of political irrelevance rooted in the mantra of professionalism that inveighed against connecting higher education to the public realm or scholarship to larger social issues, but also an attempt to convince intellectuals that their own participation in the public realm should never take place at the expense of their artistic, intellectually rigorous, or theoretically inclined skills. In this instance, the meaning of what it meant to be a public intellectual could not serve as an excuse for an anti-intellectualism that easily separates commitment from scholarship. Nor is it an excuse to substitute a celebrity-like, public-relations posturing for the important work of collective struggle and intervention. In what follows, I want to take Bourdieu's emphasis on the role of academics as public intellectuals seriously; but rather than simply defend that role I want to explore how it might be made more concrete through a related political and pedagogical engagement with the related crisis of neoliberalism and the war against youth.

I believe that academics have a particularly important role to play as engaged public intellectuals at this particular moment in history. The most dangerous problem they now face is the spread of neoliberalism, with its all consuming emphasis on market relations, commercialisation, privatisation, and the creation of a worldwide economy of part-time workers. As society is defined through the culture, values, and relations of neoliberalism, the relationship between a critical education, public morality, and civic responsibility as a condition for creating thoughtful and engaged citizens is sacrificed all too willingly to the interest of finance capital and the logic of profit-making. Under the reign of neoliberalism, citizens lose their public voice as market liberties replace civic freedoms and society increasingly depends on 'consumers to do the work of citizens' (Barber, 2001: 65). Similarly, as corporate culture extends even deeper into the basic institutions of civil and political society, there is a simultaneous diminishing of non-commodified public spheres – those institutions such as public schools, churches, non-commercial public broadcasting, libraries, trade unions and various voluntary institutions engaged in dialogue, education, and learning – that address the relationship of the self to public life and social responsibility to the broader demands of citizenship as well as provide a robust vehicle for public participation and democratic citizenship. As Herman and McChesney (1997: 3) observe, such non-commodified public spheres have played an invaluable role historically 'as places and forums where issues of importance to a political community are discussed and debated, and where information is presented that is essential to citizen participation in community life'. Without these critical public spheres corporate power often goes unchecked and politics becomes dull, cynical, and oppressive (see Giroux, 2001 for further dicussion of these issues). But more importantly, in the absence of such public spheres it becomes more difficult for citizens to challenge the neoliberal myth that citizens are *merely* consumers and that 'wholly unregulated markets are the sole means by which we can produce and distribute everything we care about, from durable goods to spiritual values, from capital development to social justice, from profitability to sustainable environments, from private wealth to essential commonweal' (Barber, 2001: 59). As democratic values give way to commercial values, intellectual ambitions are often reduced to an instrument of the entrepreneurial self, and social visions are dismissed as hopelessly out of date. Public space is portrayed exclusively as an investment opportunity, and the public good increasingly becomes a metaphor for public disorder, that is, as any notion of the public becomes synonymous with disrepair, danger, and risk, for example, public schools, public transportation, public parks, and so on. Within this discourse, anyone who does not believe that rapacious capitalism is the only road to freedom and the good life is dismissed as either a crank or worse.

In the absence of such public spaces, it has become much easier for advocates of neoliberalism to eliminate the most basic social provisions of the welfare state, weaken the power of unions, enhance the influence of corporate power over all aspects of daily life, wage war on the environment, leave citizens isolated and disarmed in the face of a worldwide culture of insecurity and fear, and wage class and racial warfare against the poor, immigrants, and people of colour. All of these are issues that academics must address as part of a pedagogy of responsibility and a politics of commitment. But what is most alarming as a result of the spread of neoliberalism, particularly in the US, is the way in which the modernist social contract that connected adult responsibility to the welfare of youth and a belief in the future has been ruptured. Traditionally, the liberal, democratic social contract occupied a defining feature of politics and was organised around a commitment which stipulated that all levels of government would assume a large measure of responsibility for providing the resources, social provisions, security and modes of education that simultaneously offered young people a future as it expanded the meaning and depth of a substantive democracy. In many respects, youth not only registered symbolically the importance of modernity's claim to progress, they also affirmed the importance of the liberal, democratic tradition of the social contract in which adult responsibility was expressed through a willingness to fight for the rights of children, enact reforms that invest in their future, and provide the educational conditions necessary for them to make use of the freedoms they have, while learning how to be critical and engaged citizens. Within such a modernist project – contradictions and damaged actualities not withstanding – democracy was measured in accordance with the well-being of youth, while the status of how a society imagined democracy and its future was contingent on how it viewed its responsibility towards future generations.

But the category of youth did more than affirm modernity's social contract rooted in a conception of the future in which adult commitment and intergenerational solidarity were articulated as a vital public service, it also affirmed those vocabularies, values and social relations central to a politics capable of both defending vital institutions as a public good, and contributing to the quality of public life. Such a vocabulary was particularly important for higher education, which often defined its highest ideals through the recognition that how it educated youth was connected to the democratic future it hoped for and its claim as an important democratic public sphere. If the connection between politics and education was tenuous in the past, youth as a symbol of the future at least provided a political and ethical referent for engaging pedagogy as a language of critique and possibility, a language that harboured an obligation to and provided the conditions for a future informed the principles of social justice and democratic values.

With the election of George W. Bush as the President of the United States, the forces of neoliberalism have become more intensified. On almost every political, economic, cultural and educational front, the market forces of privatisation, deregulation, finance capital, and capital accumulation are radically altering the national and global landscape. Political indifference on the part of the American public is now turning to political concern mediated by fear and resistance as a result of the nuclear build-up of North Korea , the war and occupation of Iraq, and the role of the United States as the single most powerful nation in the pursuit of an economic and political global empire – with occasional reference to the ongoing threat to civil liberties.

Yet, at the dawn of the new millennium, it appears that the United States no longer believes in youth, the future, or the social contract, even in its minimalist version. Since the Reagan/Thatcher revolution of the 1980s, we have been told that there is no such thing as society. And, indeed, institutions committed to public welfare have been disappearing ever since. Rather than being cherished as a symbol of hope for the future, youth are now scorned, viewed as both a worry and a nuisance, a threat to be feared and a problem to be contained. A seismic change has taken place in which youth are now being framed as a generation of shiftless, riff-raff, thugs, or potential terrorists and, hence, a threat to public life. If youth once symbolised the moral necessity to address a range of social and economic ills, they are now largely portrayed as the source of most of society's problems, condemned for violence, drugs, crime, and – if the recent spate of government sponsoredanti-drug television ads are to be believed – for terrorism as well. Hence, youth now constitute a crisis that has less to do with improving the future than with denying it. This lack of concern for the health, rights, and quality of children's lives provides the ideological and structural coherence that underlies neoliberal capitalism and its various expressions both at home and globally. The devaluation of children runs through various government policies that have shaped the last two decades. Increasingly, children are subject to a contradiction in the larger social order that reveals not only the social Darwinian nature of a society that wants to abandon anyone who is not viable economically (either as a producer or consumer) and consigns the less technologically viable to low-wage, unskilled work, but also discloses the degree to which American society has lapsed into a kind of barbarism measured by the growing refusal to pay attention to the needs of its children. The contradiction is most evident in the ongoing suppression of children's rights, the repression of their voices, and their growing status as either a threat or as simply disposable. In this context, children are viewed as unfit to be free agents and utterly infantalised, reduced to being completely dependent on adults (cf. Bauman, 1998: 83–98[1]). At the same time, when adult society wants to punish children, they are treated as adults and subject to the most brutal mechanisations of the criminal justice system, including incarceration in adult prisons and the possibility of having the death penalty imposed on them.

Youth are banished from the concerns of the moral community because they are viewed as disposable and unproductive, and their fate is not unlike that of the new poor who under the reign of neoliberalism are banished from visibility as they are removed from the discourse of deprivation to the language of depravity. Bauman's (1998: 93) comments about the poor in present day society extend to those youth that society has chosen not to invest in. He observes:

> While banishing the poor from the streets, one can also banish them from the community of humans, from the world of ethical duty. This is done by rewriting the story from the language of deprivation to that of depravity. The poor supply the 'usual suspects' rounded up to the accompaniment of public hue and cry whenever a fault in the habitual order is detected. The poor are portrayed as lax, sinful and devoid of moral standards. The media cheerfully cooperate with the police in presenting the sensation-greedy public lurid pictures of the crime–, drug– and sexual promiscuity–infested 'criminal elements' who find their shelter in the darkness of mean streets.

While youth no longer provide the referent for thinking about the future, many academics are once again engaging the sphere of the political. The future and its relationship to democracy has become a matter of great urgency for many academics because of the intensified threat posed by the Bush administration to civil liberties, unilateral aggression against Iraq, or the issue of globalisation. Unfortunately, while a great many academics have entered into a public debate around the role of the US in world affairs, the potential war with Iraq, and the ongoing repression of civil liberties, they have had almost nothing to say about how these issues affect youth. Youth rarely figure into any of the public dialogue about the curtailing of civil rights and liberties, the dismantling of big government services, the rise of the security state, and the profound changes that are driving globalisation and US imperialism. Yet, children make up 40% of the world's population and are one of the most important threads connecting matters of war, repression and empire. They are the population, after all, who will fight and die in war.

The contributions of Herman, Chomsky and a few others notwithstanding, there is almost no mention of how children figure into debates about empire, war and foreign policy. For example, the moral quality of US foreign policy is rarely invoked in reference to the enormous suffering and deaths it has imposed on the children of Iraq as a result of the US bombing in 1991 and the sanctions imposed after the war. During the 1991 war, Iraq lost a substantial part of its electrical grid, which serviced equipment in its water and sewerage plants. Of the 20 electric generating plants over 17 had been damaged and 11 were completely destroyed. One consequence was the breakdown of water, sewerage, and hospital services and the spread of various water contaminated diseases such as dysentery. Anupama Roa Singh, one of the country directors for UNICEF, has claimed that over 500,000 Iraqi children under the age of 5 have died since the imposition of UN sanctions over a decade ago. The BBC reported in 1998 that 4000 to 5000 children in Iraq are dying every month from treatable diseases that are spreading because of bad diets, and the aforementioned breakdown of the public infrastructure. Against this murderous reality, it becomes more difficult to mount a convincing humanitarian argument for the current US intervention and occupation of Iraq not only because it's clear that the murder and suffering of the children of Iraq will be intensified as a result of such actions, but also because it undercuts any moral discourse that the United States uses to defend such a war. In an impassioned speech before the US Senate, Senator Robert Byrd raised this issue with incisive clarity. He perceptively noted 'I must truly question the judgement of any President who can say that a massive unprovoked military attack on a nation which is over 50% children (under the age of 15) is "in the highest moral traditions of our country"' (Byrd, 2003). Bush's talk about the moral and democratic imperative to promote regime change, eliminate the axis of evil, and bring freedom to Iraq (and any other country the US opposes) strikes a cruel and hypocritical note in light of the role the US has played in the death of over 500,000 children in Iraq. And is it not be the same population – the people the Bush administration wants to free – who are paying the ultimate price for the current war. A recent study, 'The impact of war on Iraqi children,' claims that children under 18 – 13 million in all – are 'at a grave risk of starvation, disease, death and psychological trauma,' and that they are worse off under the current occupation by US forces than they were just before the outbreak of war in 1991. According to a study published by the United Nations Children's Fund, the recent US invasion 'has worsened the health hazards, disrupting clean water supplies, damaging sewage systems and halting rubbish collections' (BBC, 2003). Astonishingly, government officials are willing to defend the slaughter of children as politically expedient. For instance, Madeleine Albright, former US Secretary of State under Bill Clinton, appeared on the news programme, '60 Minutes' on May 12, 1996 and was asked the following question by the show's host, Leslie Stahl: 'We have heard that a half a million children have died [because of sanctions against Iraq]. I mean that's more children than died in Hiroshima. And – you know, is the price worth it?' Albright responded: 'I think this is a very hard choice, but the price – we think the price is worth it.' How might the parents of Iraqi children feel about this type of cruel political expediency? Does regime change mean that Iraqi civilians, especially children, should be targeted as part of a military and political strategy?

The moral insensitivity and inhumanity that underlies US policy towards Iraq cannot be reduced simply to the expediency of its anti-terrorism campaign or its need to seize Iraq's rich oil reserves. The roots of this indifference to the rights and needs of children, if not human life in general, must be understood within the larger framework of neoliberalism. As both an economic policy and political strategy, neoliberalism refuses to sustain the social wage, destroys those institutions that maintain social provisions, privatises all aspects of the public good, and narrows the role of the state to both a gatekeeper for capital and a policing force for maintaining social order and racial control. As an economic policy, neoliberalism allows a handful of private interests to control all aspects of society, and defines society exclusively through the privileging of market relations, deregulation, privatisation and consumerism. As a political philosophy, neoliberalism construes profit making as the essence of democracy and provides a rationale for a handful of private interests to control as much of social life as possible to maximise their financial investments. Unrestricted by social legislation or government regulation, market relations as they define the economy are viewed as a paradigm for democracy itself. Central to neoliberal philosophy is the claim that the development of all aspects of society should be left to the wisdom of the market. Similarly, neoliberal warriors argue that democratic values be subordinated to economic considerations, social issues be translated as private considerations, part-time labour replace full-time work, trade unions be weakened, and everybody be treated as a customer. Within this market-driven perspective, the exchange of capital takes precedence over social justice, the making of socially responsible citizens, and the building of democratic communities. Neoliberalism not only separates politics from economic power, destroys the public sector, and transforms everything in the image of the market, it also obliterates public concerns and cancels out the democratic impulses and practices of civil society by either devaluing or absorbing them within the logic of the market. This is what Milton Friedman, the reigning guru of neoliberalism, means in *Capitalism and Freedom* when he argues that 'the basic problem of social organization is how to co-ordinate the economic activities of large numbers of people' (Friedman, 2002: 12). There is no language here for recognising anti-democratic forms of power, developing non-market values, or fighting against substantive injustices in a society founded on deep inequalities. Hence, it is not surprising that Friedman (2002: 33) can argue without irony that he does not 'believe in freedom for madmen or children'. Nor should it be surprising that under neoliberalism children are considered valuable only in the most reductive economic terms.

The debate about repression has also failed to acknowledge how the weakening of civil liberties and basic freedoms has impacted youth and how it is related to the ongoing war against young people. While the official discourse about highjacking civic freedoms drapes itself in the mantle of national security, secrecy, and patriotism, the repressive policies that underlie the rhetoric was alive and well long before the terrorists attacks on 11th September. The short list includes the Palmer raids of the 1920s, the internment of Japanese Americans during the Second World War, the McCarthy hysteria of the 1950s, or the illegal

FBI domestic counter-intelligence programme (COINTELPRO), conducted between 1956 and 1971, whose sole purpose was to 'neutralize' politically dissident groups such as the anti-war and civil rights movements, let alone the Black Panthers. These are powerful examples of how repression has rarely been on the side of either security or justice, but what must be added to this often cited historical record are the various modes of repression that youth have been experiencing since the 1980s.

As the social contract between adult society and children disappears, the old ideology of public investment and social renewal has given way increasingly to pure repression. For instance, children, especially youth of colour, are increasingly portrayed as a danger to society and the consequences can be seen in the stepped-up application of profiling, especially among urban youth, the widespread use of random drug testing of public school students, physical searches, and the increased presence of police and the application of zero tolerance laws in the schools. As the state is increasingly reconfigured as a conduit for the criminal justice system, it withdraws from its liberal role of investing in the social and now punishes those young people who are caught in the downward spiral of its economic policies. Punishment, incarceration, and surveillance have come to represent the role of the new state. One consequence is that the implied contract between the state and citizens is broken, and social guarantees for youth as well as civic obligations to the future vanish from the agenda of public concern. Crucial issues such as homelessness, poverty, and illiteracy among youth are now viewed as individual rather than social problems and young people who have to bear the burden of their effects are now blamed for their troubles and treated as criminals rather than as victims. In a society deeply troubled by their presence, youth prompt a public rhetoric of fear, control, and surveillance, which translates into social policies that signal the shrinking of democratic public spheres, the highjacking of civic culture, and the increasing militarisation of public space. Nurturance, trust, and respect now give way to disdain and suspicion. In many suburban malls, young people, especially urban youth of colour, are subject to rigid curfew laws, gang sweeps, and cannot shop or walk around without having the appropriate identification cards or being accompanied by a parent. Children have fewer rights than almost any other group and fewer institutions protecting these rights. Moreover, they are being incarcerated at record levels and in some cases put to death. For a third of all minority youth, the future holds the disturbing possibility of either 'prison, probation, or some form of supervision within the criminal justice system' (Donziger, 1996: 101). Until the recent recession, states were spending more on prison construction than on higher education. Street (2001: 25) states that in Illinois, for every 'African-American enrolled in [its] universities, two and a-half Blacks are in prison or on parole. ... [While] in New York ... more Blacks entered prison just for drug offenses than graduated from the state's massive university system with undergraduate, masters, and doctoral degrees combined in the 1990s.' Under such circumstances, repressive practices cannot be simply linked to the war on terrorism. On the contrary, repressive policies and practices are simply reinforced and extended through an appeal to national security, but the roots of such repression lie in the spreading of neoliberalism and its transformation of the democratic state into the corporate state, and political power largely into a force for domestic militarisation and repression. Engaging the relationship between repression and the war on children expands opportunities on the part of critics and activists for understanding the current attack on civil liberties as part of a broader crisis over the political and ethical importance of the social sphere and the possibility of upholding, if not struggling, over the very idea of a democratic future both nationally and internationally.

With few exceptions, debates about globalisation also seem to take place in a world without children. And, yet, the massive changes prompted by globalisation have had a profound affect on many of the world's 2.9 billion children. In a new world order marked by deregulation, acceleration, free-flowing global finance, trade, and capital, short-term gains replace long-term visions. The search for markets and profits are now buttressed by highly destructive and sophisticated military technologies that work in conjunction with new global information systems that overcome the burden of geographical distance while creating ruling elites that no longer feel either committed or obligated to traditional notions of place, whether they be towns, cities, states, or nations. Reality TV with its social Darwinistic logic supplies the fodder for high television ratings as it provides global audiences with models of social justice repackaged as laws of nature and citizenship as an utterly privatised affair. Neoliberal globalisation widens the gap between both the public and the private, on the one hand, and politics and economic power on the other. Globalisation now signals the retreat of nation states that once played a significant role in ameliorating the most brutal features of capitalism. As the nation state abdicates its traditional hold on power, (see Marcuse, 2000, who argues that the state under neoliberal globalisation does not lack power, it abdicates power) it is being replaced by the national security state engaged in both fighting the alleged threats from domestic terrorism – signaled by an over-the-top racial profiling and anti-youth repression – and external terrorism largely manifested in the most blatant forms of racism and xenophobia directed at Arab and Muslim populations and immigrants. The consequences of neoliberal globalisation can be seen not only in growing inequalities worldwide in income, wealth, basic services, and health care, but also in substantial increases in the exploitation and suffering of millions of children around the globe. The fallout is easy to document. As globalisation and militarisation mutually reinforce each other as both an economic policy and as a means to settle conflicts, wars are no longer fought between soldiers but are now visited upon civilians and appear to have the most detrimental effects on children. Within the last decade, two million children have died in military conflicts. Another four million have been disabled, 12 million have been left homeless, and millions more have been orphaned (UNICEF, 2003). Increasingly, children are being recruited, abducted, or forced into military service as lighter weapons enable children as young as 12 to be trained as effective killers. But the fruits of modern warfare not only enable children to kill, they also result in their deaths, especially through the proliferation of landmines, which are estimated to kill 8000 to 10,000 children each year. The International Committee on the Red Cross estimates that 'some 110 million land mines threaten children in more than 70 countries' and that they are chillingly effective: '82.5 percent of amputations performed in ICRC hospitals are for land mine victims' (Sutton-Redner, 2002).

As the leading supplier of arms in the world, the United States bears an enormous responsibility for fuelling military conflicts throughout the globe. As reported in the Congressional Research Service, a division of the Library of Congress, American manufacturers in 2000 signed contracts for just under $18.6 billion in weapon sales, with sales going primarily to developing countries. Empire in this instance is not simply about the power pretensions of an imperial presidency, it is also about neoliberal policies that feed corporate profits through the selling of arms that largely kill and maim children. Hence, it should come as no surprise to learn that in the age of empire, domestic markets even in the United States are no longer at a safe remove from the scorched earth policies and consequences of arms manufacturers. For instance, the United States ranks worst among industrialised nations in the number of children killed by guns, with over 50,000 American youth killed since 1979. Globalisation is not only about the emergence of new technologies, the consolidation of corporate power, and the flow of financial capital, it is also about the intersection of profits and militarisation – and the killing and maiming of poor children at home and abroad. Under such circumstances, it makes more sense for left critics to address the issue of globalisation and Bush's 'Axis of Evil' moralism by exposing the administration's hypocrisy in promoting the conditions for military conflict all over the globe. In spite of what the cheerleaders for neoliberalism claim, globalisation is not simply about creating 'free trade' and opening markets. In actuality, it refers to 'advancing ... corporate and commercial interests' (McChesney, 2001: 16) through the internationalisation of armed conflict and globalisation policies fuelled by the incessant need for profits whatever the human costs.

The division of labour and exploitation promoted through neoliberal globalisation has given new meaning to Castells' (1998: 149) pronouncement that the primary labour issue in the new information age 'is not the end of work but the condition of work'.[2] The search for cheap labour, the powerlessness of children, and the 120 million children who are born poor each year create fertile conditions for multinational corporations to gain significant profits through the hiring of children, largely in developing countries. The International Labor Office estimates that 120 million children between the ages of 5 and 14 are compelled to work full time, often under harsh and inhumane conditions, and that if part-time work is included the figure reaches 250 million (ILO, 2003). Children are engaged in a variety of forms of labour ranging from domestic servants and shoe production to brick making and agricultural work. Many children are either injured or killed on the job, with the number of annual injuries estimated at 70,000. Not all children are exploited by being paid sub-standard wages for their work; the most unfortunate, and generally the most destitute, are forced into bonded slavery in order to pay off their family loans or are sold outright on the market by their families in the hopes of bringing in additional income. Many of these children are forced into prostitution, domestic service, or put on the streets as beggars. What is particularly alarming is the growing market of children as sexual commodities driven on by the globalisation of child pornography rings largely circulated through the Internet and other global circuits of power such as organised sex tours. While the figures on this illicit trade are difficult to establish, it has been estimated by the Center for Protection of Children's Rights that as many as 800,000 children are in prostitution, many with HIV infections. Child prostitution is also on the rise in the United States, with an estimated

100,000 to 300,000 children exploited through prostitution and pornography (World Congress against Commercial Sexual Exploitation of Children, 1996: 70). In spite of the virtual crisis that children are facing all over the world with respect to the violation of their rights and their bodily dignity, the United States has refused to both address critically the myriad ways in which it contributes to turning innocent children into victims through policies that strip countries of their public services, resources, and revenue while at the same time declining to ratify a number of international treaties designed specifically to improve the quality of life for the world's children. The message that is unabashedly put forth by the Bush administration about children both at home and abroad is that it has little regard for the bodies and minds of young people. This message is reinforced by a market-driven politics that suggests that children under the command of neoliberalism do not even merit a commitment to human rights, social justice, health care, or minimal social provisions. How else can we explain the refusal of the Bush administration to sign or ratify the United Nations Convention on the Rights of the Child (passed in 1989), the small arms treaty, and the land mines treaty? Moreover, the Bush administration has rejected the Kyoto Protocol on climate change, refused to sign the protocol for the Biological Weapons Convention as well as the International Covenant on Economic, Social and Cultural Rights.

The Responsibility of Intellectuals

As a public sphere that both prepares youth for the future as well as shape it, higher education is deeply implicated in how it relates to broader social, political and economic forces that bear down on youth. As the subject and object of learning, youth provide faculty and administrators with a political and moral referent for addressing the relationship between knowledge and power, learning and social change, and values and classroom social relations as they bridge the gap between the diverse public spheres that youth inhabit and the university as a site of socialisation and political engagement. The very presence of youth, particularly from the middle and upper classes, in the university raises important questions about the role of the university in furthering and reproducing those divisions of labour between the rich and the poor that are made visible not only in the presence of diverse student bodies, but which also inform a host of social formations outside the university. Educators would do well in their own classrooms and teaching to address how higher education furthers class, racial, and gender divisions and what this might mean in terms of its changing nature under the rule of neoliberalism. Surely, if educators have a responsibility to fight against those forces that undermine the university as a public sphere, they would have to address the increasing corporatisation of university life and its effects on faculty, students, and the very meaning of what it means to be educated to be a critical citizen of the world.

One of the challenges that academics face as engaged intellectuals centres around recovering the language of the social, agency, solidarity, democracy and public life as the basis for creating new conceptions of pedagogy, learning, and governance. Part of this effort demands creating new vocabularies, experiences, and subject positions that allow students to become more than they are now, to question what it is they have become within existing institutional and social formations, and 'to give some thought to their experiences so that they can transform their relations of subordination and oppression' (Worsham and Olson, 1999:178). Amin has rightly argued that it is the absence of social values such as generosity and human solidarity that 'reinforce[s] submission to the dominating power of capitalist ideology' (Amin, 2001: 16). And yet, it is precisely through a focus on the obligations that adult society has to children that such values become concrete and persuasive. It is often difficult for adults and students to dismiss the suffering of children as a matter of individual character or to reduce their plight to the realm of the family or private sphere, the depoliticising strategy of choice used by social conservatives and neoliberals. Children provide a powerful referent for a pedagogy of disruption, social criticism, and collective change because their suffering and hardships offer the pedagogical promise of both a public hearing and a potent social category to connect a range of issues and problems that are often addressed in isolation, a subtle way of identifying grievances without inquiring into their social and political roots. More than any other group, they provide a credible referent for challenging the moralisms of conservatives while simultaneously opening up the possibility to create new ethical discourses, modes of agency, and forms of advocacy. Children are one of the few referents left for reclaiming a future that does not imitate the present, a future that makes good on the promise of new models of human association and pedagogy based on democratic values and a radical transformation of the existing inegalitarian structures of political power and economic wealth. A social analysis of the role of children is not only important for its own sake, but also because it points to a much larger social analysis in that the various forms of oppression that children experience directly undermines the dominant and traditional justifications for larger class, racial, sexual, and gendered divisions in society. The emphasis on children's experience is important here because it foregrounds the relationship between power and the lived realities shaped by material relations of power. More specifically, children provide a more crucial way to analyse hegemony. That is, hegemony in this instance does not simply refer to the ideologies, discourses, or images that represent children or position them in particular ways, but also to the way in which they actually experience the different modalities of power and powerlessness as an empirical reality within particular class and racial formations marked by deep inequalities of power (Crehan, 2002: 202–207). Children are born into the existing social order and cannot be blamed so easily for the conditions of poverty, racism, and daily violence that produce inadequate health care, education, and housing for the most defenceless and least powerful of its inhabitants. The oppression of children is crucial for public intellectuals to address because it is the fundamental lie at the heart of neoliberalism and its falsely 'utopian' notion of the future. The plight of children must play a central role in rearticulating the promise of critical citizenship and reaffirmation of a social contract that embraces and affirms democratic values, practices, and identities while challenging the limitations of those individualizsing relations and identities produced by neoliberalism. The social position of children cannot help but challenge the core ideology of neoliberalism.

Educators need a new language in which children are not detached from politics but become central to any transformative notion of pedagogy conceived in terms of social and public responsibility. The growing attack on youth in American society may say less about the reputed apathy of the populace than it might about the bankruptcy of old political languages and orthodoxies and the need for new vocabularies and visions for clarifying our intellectual, ethical and political projects, especially as they work to reabsorb questions of agency, ethics, and meaning back into politics and public life. In the absence of such a language and the social formations and public spheres that make democracy and justice operative, politics becomes narcissistic and caters to the mood of widespread pessimism and the cathartic allure of the spectacle. In addition, public service and government intervention is sneered upon as either bureaucratic or a constraint upon individual freedom. Any attempt to give new life to a substantive democratic politics suggests that educators address the issue of both how people learn to be political agents and what kind of educational work is necessary within what kind of public spaces to enable people to use their full intellectual resources to provide a profound critique of existing institutions and struggle to make the operation of freedom and autonomy possible for as many people as possible in a wide variety of spheres. As critical educators, we are required to understand more fully why the tools we used in the past feel awkward in the present, often failing to respond to problems now facing the United States and other parts of the globe. More specifically, educators face the challenge posed by the failure of existing critical discourses to bridge the gap between how society represents itself and how and why individuals fail to understand and critically engage such representations in order to intervene in the oppressive social relationships they often legitimate. At a time when civil liberties are being destroyed, Iraq is under American occupation, and public institutions and goods all over the globe are under assault by the forces of a rapacious global capitalism, there is a sense of concrete urgency that demands not only the most militant forms of political opposition on the part of academics, but new modes of resistance and collective struggle buttressed by rigorous intellectual work, social responsibility, and political courage. The time has come for intellectuals to distinguish caution from cowardice and recognise that their obligations extend beyond deconstructing texts or promoting a culture of questioning. These are important pedagogical interventions, but they do not go far enough. We also need to link knowing with action, learning with social engagement, and this suggests addressing the responsibilities that come with teaching students to fight for an inclusive and radical democracy by recognising that pedagogy is not just about understanding, however critical, but also provides the conditions for addressing the responsibilities we have as citizens to others, especially those who will inherit the future.

Pedagogy plays a crucial role in nurturing this type of responsibility and suggests that students should learn about the relevance of translating critique and understanding to civic courage, of translating what they know as a matter of private privilege into a concern for public life. Responsibility breathes politics into educational practices and suggests both a different future and the possibility of politics itself. Responsibility makes politics and agency possible, because it does not end with matters of understanding since it recognises the importance of students becoming accountable for others through their ideas, language, and actions. Being aware of the conditions that cause human suffering and the deep inequalities that generate dreadfully undemocratic and unethical contradictions for many people is not the same as resolving them. If pedagogy is to be linked to critical citizenship and public life, it needs to provide the conditions for students to learn in diverse ways how to take responsibility for moving society in the direction of a more realisable democracy. In this case, the burden of pedagogy is linked to the possibilities of understanding and acting, engaging knowledge and theory as a resource to enhance the capacity for civic action and democratic change. As Derrida (2000: 9) reminds us, democracy 'demands the most concrete urgency ... because as a concept it makes visible the promise of democracy, that which is to come'. But for educators to recognise the urgency of the crisis that links youth and democracy they will have to betray those dominant intellectual traditions that divorce academic life from politics, reduce teaching to forms of instrumental rationality that largely serve market interests, and remove the university from those democratic values that hold open the promise of a better and more humane life.

Correspondence

Any correspondence should be directed to Professor Henry A. Giroux, Waterbury Chair Professor, 217 Chambers Bldg, Penn State University, University Park, PA 16803, USA (HAG5@psu.edu).

Notes

1. Bauman provides the same sort of analysis in describing the state of the poor under neoliberalism. He argues that the poor are excluded and often charged with the guilt of their exclusion, and thus seen as dangerous and a threat to society.
2. Of course, while Castells is right about the conditions of labour, he under-emphasises the huge surplus of labour around the world. This is made clear in another ILO report, which states that about a quarter of the labour force around the world is unemployed and a third are underemployed.

References

Amin, S. (2001) Imperialization and globalization. *Monthly Review* (June 2001).
Barber, B.R. (2001) Blood brothers, consumers, or citizens? Three models of identity – ethnic, commercial, and civic. In C. Gould and P. Pasquino (eds) *Cultural Identity and the Nation State*. Lanham: Rowman and Littlefield.
Bauman, Z. (1998) *Work, Consumerism and the New Poor*. Philadelphia: Open University Press.
BBC (2003) Child sickness 'soars' in Iraq, 9th June 2003. On WWW at http://commondreams.org/headlines03/0609-05.htm.
Bourdieu, P. (2000) For a scholarship with commitment. *Profession 2000*.
Byrd, R. (2003) Reckless administration may reap disastrous consequences, Senate Floor Speech, 12 February 2003. On WWW at http://www.commondreams.org/views03/0212-07.htm.
Castells, M. (1998) *End of Millennium, III*. Malden, MA: Balckwell.
Crehan, K. (2002) *Gramasci, Culture, and Anhtropology*. Los Angeles: University of California Press.
Derrida, J. (2000) Intellectual courage: An interview (trans P. Krapp). *Culture Machine* (Vol. 2).
Donziger, S.R. (ed.) (1996) *The Real War on Crime: The Report of the National Criminal Justice Commission*. New York: Harper Perennial.
Friedman, M. (2002) *Capitalism and Freedom*. Chicago: University of Chicago Press.

Giroux, H.A. (2001) *Public Spaces, Private Lives: Beyond the Culture of Cynicism.* Lanham: Rowman and Littlefield.

Herman, E.S. and McChesney, R.W. (1997) *The Global Media: The New Missionaries of Global Capitalism.* Washington: Cassell.

ILO (International Labor Office) (July 2003) *Child Labor 101.* On WWW at http://us.ilo.org/ilokidsnew /ILOU/101.html.

Marcuse, P. (2000) The language of globalization. *Monthly Review* 52 (3). On WWW at http://www.monthlyreview.org/700marc.htm.

McChesney, R.W. (2001) Global media, neoliberalism, and imperialism. *Monthly Reveiw* (March 2001).

Stabile, C.A. and Morooka, J. (2003) Between two evils, I refuse to choose the lesser. *Cultural Studies* 17 (3).

Street, P. (2001) Race, prison, and poverty: The race to incarcerate in the age of correctioanl Keynesianism. *Z Magazine* (May 2001).

Sutton-Redner, J. (2002) Children in a world of violence. *Children in Need Magazine* (December 2002). On WWW at http://childreninneed.com/magazine /violence/html.

UNICEF (2003) *The State of the World's Children 2003.* On WWW at http://www.unicef.org/sowc03.

World Congress against Commercial Sexual Exploitation of Children (1996) End child prostitution, child pornography, and the trafficking of children for sexual exploitation (ECPAT). *Europe and North America Regional Profile.* Stockholm.

Worsham, L. and Olson, G.A. (1999) Rethinking political community: Chantal Mouffe's liberal socialism. *Journal of Composition Theory* 19 (2).

Wright Edelman, M. Standing up for the world's children: Leave no child behind. On WWW at http://gos.sbc.edu/e/edelman.html.

2 Academic Literacy in Post-colonial Times: Hegemonic Norms and Transcultural Possibilities

Joan Turner
Goldsmiths College, University of London, UK

In this paper, I argue that it is important to bring proficiency in written English language into the frame of a critical pedagogy for academic literacy. This may at first seem a counter-intuitive goal with connotations of constraint and convergence rather than opening up and diversity. However, what is often not taken into account in the notion of opening up new spaces of critique or new 'languages' is that those new critical 'languages' operate in a dominant materially concrete, linguistic language, namely English. The opportunity to manipulate the representational resources of English therefore is a necessary pedagogical goal if one wants to open up participation in academic literacy practices to a wider selection of people than is currently the case. By on the one hand, raising awareness of subjectification into the rhetorical norms of academic writing by pointing up their historical construction, and on the other, looking at an example of a Korean PhD student working with the theoretical discourses of post-colonialism and psychoanalysis in English, I hope to refigure the prevailing assumptions on attention to form in written English.

탈식민지 시대의 아카데믹 교양성:헤게모니적 규범과 간문화적 가능성

이 글에서 나는 영어쓰기에 있어 "숙련됨"을 학술 교양성의 비판적 교육 방법론의 틀내로 들여와야 한다고 주장한다. 이 주장은 당장 개방성과 다양성보다는 구속과 집중을 의미하는 그리 상식에 반하는 목표처럼 들릴수도 있다. 그러나 새로운 비판성 혹은 새로운 언어를 위한 공간 개방등의 개념을 설명할때 자주 언급되지 않는 사실은 그런 새로운 비판적 언어조차도 영어라고 하는 지배적으로 물질적이며 구체적인 언어학적 언어내에서 작동된다고 하는 점이다. 만약 우리가 지금보다 더 다양한 부류의 사람들에게 학술 교양 연습에 참여하는 것을 개방하려 한다면 영어로 된 표현 자료를 조작하는 기회는 고로 필수적 교육 목표라고 하겠다. 한편으로 학술적 글쓰기의 수사적 규범을 주체화하는 과정에 대한 인식을 역사적 구성주의라는 관점에서 제고하고, 다른 한편으로 탈식민지 주의론와 정신분석학의 이론적 담론의 선상에서 작업하는 한국출신의 박사과정 학생을 예로 들며, 씌어진 영어의 형식에 대한 관심에 팽배한 가정들을 재구성하고자 한다.

The Historical Construction of Rhetorical Norms for Academic Literacy

In this section, I want to look at academic literacy as a historically constructed rhetorical practice, invested with norms and values which are the result of the rise to prominence of scientific rationality and the European Enlightenment's desire for universal knowledge. These may also be seen as the norms and values which shaped and were shaped by what Foucault (1970) called the 'classical episteme'. They include the subject position of a supremely rational Cartesian 'cogito'; that of an 'ideal observer', whose observations are precise and 'objective'; and a relationship of mastery between 'man' and knowledge, and particularly European 'man' and its Others.

Within critical pedagogy, Giroux (1992) has critiqued the binary opposition between 'clarity' and 'complexity' that has thwarted the take-up of contemporary theorising in educational discourse. This debate has been waged particularly strongly in the USA where, to summarise, complex theorising has been resisted for its lack of clarity, and pragmatic issues of practice have been foregrounded instead. I would like here also to focus on clarity, but not to promote it in contradistinction to complexity. Rather I'd like to deconstruct it, to show its embeddedness in the roots of knowledge production practices at the time of the European Enlightenment, and its subsequent valorisation as a rhetorical norm, or rather a collection of rhetorical norms. I would agree with Giroux that the use of 'clarity' as a common-sense requirement constitutes 'a troublesome politics of erasure by claiming to represent a universal standard of literacy' (1992: 24) but want in this way to show that this is an effect of power in knowledge production practices. Historicising 'clarity' therefore goes some way to dislodging the complacency that goes with treating it as 'common sense'.

The importance of clarity and precision as intellectual cultural values may be traced back to the 17th century and Descartes' insistence on the importance of 'clear and distinct' ideas. As Cottingham (1988: 32) writes:

> Descartes insisted that no concept should be allowed in a philosophical or scientific explanation unless it is either transparently clear or capable of being reduced by analysis to elements that are clear.

While Descartes may be seen as epitomising the importance of the rational, the 'cogito', in England at around the same time, importance was being placed on empirical findings. The emphasis on empiricism brought with it a fear that language might not be used adequately enough to convey the exactitude of the scientific knowledge that was so prolifically being 'discovered' at the time. By using language as they were wont to use it in their everyday lives, people were in danger of 'distorting' the communication of hallowed knowledge. This fear of using language improperly may be seen in the following quote from Locke's *Essay Concerning Human Understanding*:

> For Language being the great Conduit, whereby Men convey their discoveries, Reasonings and Knowledge, from one to another, he that makes an ill use of it, though he does not corrupt the Fountains of Knowledge, which are in Things themselves; yet he does, as much as in him lies, break or stop the Pipes, whereby it is distributed to the publick use and advantage of Mankind. (1689, Book III. Chapter 11, Section 5: quoted in Harris & Taylor, 1997: 127).

This quote also instantiates the conduit metaphor for communication whose enduring influence is evidenced in Reddy's (1979) account. Reddy estimates that the conduit metaphor accounts for 70% of all expressions conceptualising communication. Such expressions include: 'getting the message across' and 'putting things into words'. The success of the conduit metaphor may itself be seen as the filtering of political/conceptual power into the linguistic resources of the lexicon. It was helpful to empirical philosophers and scientists to 'discipline' language by making it perform as a vehicle of communication, transmitting directly from the minds of the scientists, or from what was minutely observed, to the audience of patrons, politicians, and fellow scientists of the time. Attempts to even more rigidly constrain language use by creating artificial languages such as Leibniz's 'algebra of thought' or Bishop Wilkins' 'Real Character' did not succeed. The continuing prevalence of the conduit metaphor in expressions for communication may be seen as one example of power rhetoricised in language. The expectations of rhetorical norms in writing, what Giroux calls a 'stylised aesthetic of clarity' (1992: 25) may be seen as another.

Newton's Visibilising Rhetoric

Bazerman's (1988) account of Newton honing his rhetorical strategies to the socio-political demands of his time, thereby creating a new epistemic reality, may be seen as another example of the embedding of rhetorical norms which became normative, and whose normative power continues. Newton appealed to both the rationalists and empiricists in his peer group by relying on the deductive logic of geometrical proof, which lent generality and universality to his claims (Bazerman: 1988: 117) and by giving an account of his findings so that 'they appear as concrete fact, as real as an earthquake or ore found in Germany even though the events that made these facts visible to Newton occurred in a private laboratory as the result of speculative ponderings and active experimental manipulations' (Bazerman, 1988: 90).

Bazerman talks of Newton 'marching' the reader through 40 pages of narration and discussion, 'creating a tactile and ideal proof of the theorem' (1988: 122). In this way, Newton has successfully combined the effect of hands-on empiricism with in-the-head rationalism. A flavour of the contests between the empirical scientists, the makers of practical apparatus such as Hooke and the rationalists of whom Newton is a prime example, is given in Jardine's (1999) *Ingenious Pursuits*. Newton's visibilising rhetorical strategies, making the journey of discovery as concrete as possible, and laying things out in clearly signposted logical exposition as in a geometrical proof, parallelled the literal mapping of the world and the explanatory process of science that were key to the ethos of Europe at the time.

Newton is a prime example of how, while cartographers were mapping the world (in what is now a notoriously Eurocentric way, cf. Hall, 1992), the rhetorical mapping of knowledge was also being carried out. Rhetorical action as clearly signposted logical exposition may be seen as another product of the age. It is affected by the same confidence in 'man's' Reason, which in turn is imbued with the certainty of deductive logic.

Rhetorical Regularisation and Subjectification

Newton's *Optics* was reprinted several times and accrued status and admiration, thereby affording the opportunity for his rhetorical structuring to be replicated in different contexts and with different subject matter. Such a process need not have been consciously undertaken, but a popular text is likely to have effects on what counts as accessible style and generate norms of accessibility. In the preface to an early 20th century edition of *Optics*, Albert Einstein shows its enduring effects by praising Newton's 'joy in creation and his minute precision ... evident in every word and every figure' (quoted in Bazerman, 1988: 124).

'Minute precision' is obviously a positive evaluation and symptomatic of a range of rhetorical virtues embodying economy and elegance as well as exactitude and certainty. I encountered a similar valorisation of written style in a semi-structured interview with a PhD supervisor on the role of language use in the PhD. (JT is the interviewer, and S is the supervisor.)

S: I encourage all students to develop fluency and a degree of elegance – especially in the later stages. First language users need to develop this also.

JT: Can you be a bit more specific about what you mean by elegance?

S: Yeh - um - that is expressing for example one thought in a sentence, one particular chain of thoughts in a paragraph and an extended chain of thoughts in a section rather than – em starting one thing then going to another one or even in a sentence, starting another chain of thought. Certainly it's the ordering and presentation of thought, the more economically it's done, I think the more successful it is.

These comments chime very much with the kind of precepts found in textbooks on academic writing, developing a paragraph from a topic sentence. It seems that logical exposition, concision in choice of lexis, and economy of style continue to be the norms within which academic writing pedagogy and expectations of a smooth read, operate. This is a visibilising economy whereby the reader is led along a route of clearly identified argumentation, without detour and distraction.

In analogy with Foucault's account of the visibilising technologies of the examination and the panopticon (1973, 1977) and the subjectification that it effects on those being controlled, i.e. the way they come to police themselves, I suggest that visibilising rhetorical strategies are a disciplining technology for language use and for language users. Academic writers are subjected into this visibilising economy, and with the help of textbooks, writing pedagogies, assessment processes and the like continue to police its viability.

What is perhaps most insidious in this visibilising process is the fact that the rhetoricity itself remains invisible, as with the techniques of surveillance that Foucault (1973) recounts. The assumption is that linguistic expression will be clear, and therefore not draw attention to itself. As a result, when attention is drawn to language, as is often the case for L2 writers or those new to the cultural practice of academic literacy, they are immediately placed in deficit. Furthermore, the imbrication of language use and rationality is such that the deficit assumption does not usually only relate to deficiency in knowledge of English, but to cognitive deficiency *per se*. Such a deficit model is one which a critical pedagogy for language teaching, particularly academic writing, has to tackle, but not by ignoring the discourse of transparency (see also Lillis & Turner, 2001; Turner, 1999) in which language has been culturally constructed. Rather the hegemony of 'clarity' and the norms that go with it have to be recognised, made visible, and taught. Only then can those who want to participate in academic literacy practices find the micro-spaces where resistance can be opened up and new ways of operating be introduced.

The Ideal Observer

Many strands of contemporary cultural theorising, including post-structuralism, post-colonialism, psychoanalytical theory, deconstruction, and 'critical theory' originating from the Frankfurt school, take their cue from dismantling or refiguring the 'ideal observer' whose 'colonising gaze' has constructed the epistemic norms of Eurocentric academic discourse. For example, Nagel (1986) has termed it 'a view from nowhere', while Code (1995) in her book entitled *Rhetorical Spaces* wants to refigure or rethink what she calls the 'epistemic' subject quite differently in order 'to refuse the excesses and excuses of monologic isolationism'. Monologic isolationism is the rhetorical strategy favoured in mainstream epistemological discourses in which the 'exact sciences' have 'pride of place'. In these discourses, the epistemic subject is 'the abstract, interchangeable individual whose monologues have been spoken from nowhere, in particular, to an audience of faceless and usually disembodied onlookers' (Code, 1995: xiv).

While these and other critiques are being levelled in contemporary theorising, the rhetoricisation of the ideal observer continues apace in what constitutes academic literacy. The genre of the academic essay, for example, implicitly invites the adoption of a survey position over a particular academic terrain, through which the course of an argument has to be charted. Also, the notion of the 'topic sentence' is a mainstay of academic writing pedagogy and effectively encodes the survey position, giving an encapsulating, generalising overview, setting the scene. All of these visual and possessive metaphors are emblematic of what Pratt (1992: 7) calls the 'seeing-man', the European male subject 'whose imperial eyes passively look out and possess'. However, it is difficult to simply shrug off this embodied rhetoricity in academic writing. It is constitutive of the promotion of argumentation through a specific conceptual landscape which has to be made clear, 'visible' to a readership. In my consultations with a Korean student, excerpts of whose texts I will discuss later, my role often appeared to be as the guardian of the 'ideal observer' subject position. The following type of exchange between us was frequent:

Language Tutor: Make your sentences shorter, they are much more powerful

PhD Student: Oh but there are so many possibilities – I can't just say that. I don't want to give the impression that I have absolute knowledge or that there is just one possibility.

Her awareness of the multiplicity of possible positions and her reluctance to assert an overriding one meant that she was resisting the subjectivity of the ideal observer and the topic sentence, preferably short and sweet, as an instantiation of its rhetoricisation. In contradistinction to this overviewing position, or even of claiming her own, as it were, territorialising, position, she expressed a desire to let the issues emerge through her psychoanalytic reading of two Korean artists' work.

In support of an emergentist mode of writing, she mentioned the work of the Vietnamese feminist writer and film-maker, Trinh T. Minh-ha, who has been able to create a new way of saying things both through film and in her writings. The following is an example of Trinh's approach to writing, which she gave in conversation with Annamaria Morelli (1996: 4–5):

> When I write, I never know ahead of time where the writing is going to lead me. I never proceed by having a plan (with an introduction, a development and a conclusion, for example), by mapping out the terrain of the arguments I wish to sustain, or even by compiling ahead of time all the points I want to discuss; I never work that way.

Trinh's words could be taken as a direct refutation of conventional academic writing pedagogy. Perhaps as a feminist theoretician and thinker Trinh T. Minh-ha is deliberately espousing a different style of writing from that engendered by the masculinist style of scientific rationality. However, the problem is that the latter is the style embedded in what constitutes academic literacy. While I am sympathetic to this student's desire to invest the implications of the theoretical critiques of Eurocentric historiography into her own writing, it conflicted with the hegemony of normative academic writing and the subjectivity of the 'ideal observer' which goes with it. However, beyond the PhD, it will be possible for her to experiment with different forms of writing.

Epistemic Shifts and Rhetoricisation

As with Newton and the scientific rationality that he was helping to rhetoricise, contemporary theorising is also motivating rhetorical change. One such is the use of the pronoun 'I' which, while its use can still be problematic (see, for example, Ivanič, 1998) may stand metonymically for an 'embodied' rather than an ideal/rational subjectivity. Another rhetoricisation marking the epistemic shift in contemporary theorising from a rigorous either/or logic to an acceptance of ambiguity and indeed 'undecidability' is the use of a lexical couplet signalling the possibility of both, usually antithetical, meanings. The use of 'within/beyond' is one such and appears in the student's text as follows:

> In other words, I discuss the 'voice-symptomatic' (un)consciousness with which the sexual slave women spoke in South Korea during the 1990s which appears in the site of contestation within/beyond the 'ideological' consciousness and the state of knowledge determined by the ideologically organized normative discursive perfomative relations between Japan and Korea and its postwar political and economical relations.

While this rhetorical shift for expressing ambivalence is possible, however, the overly long sentence construction and sometimes lack of clear referents is not.

In general, however, the concrete materiality of any particular language in use, whether spoken or written, is seldom brought into discussions, even when it is clear that contemporary post-humanist, or post-colonial theorising itself is done in European languages, predominantly English. There is a gap between the critiques that are being made against the dominant epistemology of European Enlightenment thinking and the material language and its rhetorical norms in which those critiques are being made. There is a need therefore for some self-reflexivity here. However, as Venn (2000) points out with his notion of 'occidentalism', 'occidentalism recognises the impossibility of starting afresh as it were, with new conceptual frameworks but at the same time wants to go beyond the assumptions of modernity' (Venn, 2000: 156). The situation is similar with occidentalist rhetoricity. All of its norms and precepts cannot be overturned at once. It is incumbent on a critical pedagogy of academic writing, however, not to simply teach such norms as givens, but to locate them in their culturally constructed context.

Language in Post-colonial Studies

The issue of language in post-colonial studies is a very broad topic and I cannot go into it deeply here. However, its own metalanguage provides some of the more common analytical determiners for the area of study. For example, the concepts of speech and silence serve to describe, or even explain, the feelings of oppression and repression that are a large part of post-colonial experience. Hall (1996a: 117) puts this well in his description of Africa and Europe: 'where Africa was a case of the unspoken, Europe was a case of that which is endlessly speaking – and endlessly speaking *us*.' At the same time, 'Africa' was still very much alive in Caribbean culture. Hall (1996a: 116) again:

> In the everyday life and customs of the slave quarters, in the languages and patois of the plantation, in names and words, often disconnected from their taxonomies, in the secret syntactical structures through which other languages were spoken, in the stories and tales told to children, in religious practices and beliefs, in the spiritual life, the arts, crafts, musics and rhythms of slave and post-emancipation society, Africa, the signified which could not be represented directly in slavery, remained and remains the unspoken, unspeakable 'presence' in Caribbean culture. It is 'hiding' behind every verbal inflection, every narrative twist of Caribbean cultural life.

In the context of world Englishes, the creativity of different writers drawing on their cultural background has often been highlighted with the notion of 'contact literatures' e.g. Gonzalez (1987), Kachru (1987) and Parthasarathy (1987). Pratt (1992) also draws on the linguistic concept of 'contact' in her notion of 'contact zones' where transculturation processes take place. The notion of transculturation puts out the possibility of dissolving binaries. Hall (1996b) sees the situation of post-colonialism in this way, beyond the anti-colonial simplicity of the colonising and the colonised. Transculturation has also been taken up as a possible model for teaching English to speakers of other languages (cf. Zamel, 1997). Zamel (1997: 343) takes issue with 'determinism', a stance that assumes that we can attribute a student's attempts in another language to that student's L1 background and that anticipates that a student's linguistic and cultural background will be problematic and limiting. I would broadly agree with this position. However, I would like to add the notion of 'interpolation' to this model and emphasise the role that proficiency in English plays in it. The post-colonial theorist Ashcroft (2001: 57) gives the example of 'a key "interpolation" of global knowledge' whereby the Trinidadian independence leader, Eric Williams used his flair for language to expose the nature of imperial history in its treatment of the West Indies. Ashcroft (2001: 58) also talks of the concern for proper speech as a classic demonstration of cultural hegemony, but points to the ambivalence of hegemony, and states that 'mastering the master's language has been a key strategy of self empowerment in all post-colonial societies'. He affirms that 'proficiency in the language does not exclude the capacity to use it in a way that localizes it'. In the world of literacy teaching, Delpit (1998: 217) also advocates the 'liberatory ends' of teaching the 'language of the master'.

This is broadly the position that I follow here where I show excerpts from a post-graduate student's PhD thesis, where I feel that the problem is strongly the need for greater proficiency in written English. She is fully competent to explain any theoretical terms that she is working with, or to explain to me what she means when I don't understand what she is trying to say in her writing. In fact, she has no difficulty at all in spoken English. The excerpts chosen are not unusual, but rather the norm in her writing. They are complex, because the theoretical discourse she is working with, predominantly that of psychoanalysis, is complex. I would like to suggest, that because this theoretical discourse is complex, she has all the more need to focus on the English. In this way, her English-speaking readers, her supervisors, and external examiners, can focus only on her analysis. The excerpts come from a chapter of the student's thesis, entitled: The post-colonial work of memory and progress.

> It was historical necessity for Korean people to encounter with huge antagonism against the historical procession in the 1980's, given that the malise and colonislity in the society I have described earlier had persisted without resolution. The inspiration and aspiration of the time was crystallised in the word, *Jinbo* (that also means progress). *Jinbo that is coined with the term of the age* minjung *(grass root people)* summed up and used to indicate what is the ethos of this movement that is the 'progress' of those who had been hitherto repressed, subalternized and minoritized.

I do not wish to comment on the whole of this excerpt, but want to point out two things. One is that micro-level attention to the use of English would help make her argument stronger, and the other is that the use of resonant terms in the context of analysis, may be seen as an example of 'transculturation'. Her structuring, 'encounter ... against' for example, could be replaced by 'counter', and the use of 'historical procession' could be disambiguated by re-phrasing it as 'the procession of history'.

The example of transculturation comes from the use (here in transliteration, but also in the student's text in Korean ideograms) of the Korean words *jinbo*, and *minjung,* resonant with the politically charged climate in Korea of the 1980s, especially after the Kwangju shooting of civilians by government troops. The student introduces other Korean words into her thesis, and in this respect, there is no problem with the conventions of the PhD. This kind of linguistic hybridity is allowed. However, when it appears that attributes of Korean syntax, such as the non-existence of relative pronouns and prepositions (cf. Thompson, 1987), sometimes make for conflations in the student's text that need to be clausally distinct in English, this becomes a major problem. The following sentence is an example:

> The ongoing study of postcolonial subjectivity, which has been focused on the question of the identity and politics of identification but it has not been

deeply delved into the potential historicity inscribed in the postcolonial memory to reactivate it toward a creative energy.

The situation for this student was also fraught with contradictions. These lay in her desires, not only to write outside totalising discourses, but also to 'write well' be persuasive and say something fresh in her PhD, which she wanted people to take notice of. She was also quite emotionally and politically engaged with her subject matter. When I would talk of traditional academic discourse and the need for foregrounding and justification and for a general 'flow' of the argumentation, she would say 'yes I want to write like that'.

This example of student writing reflects quite a lot of the problems of identity that Ivanič (1998) highlights. The student wants to contribute to knowledge, she has a strong personal voice and wants to make what she has to say known to a wider audience, but she is constrained particularly by her 'discoursal' voice, where the discourse is shaped by the institutional demands of the PhD, which in turn is shaped by the rhetorical ideologies embedded in academic literacy practices since the European Enlightenment, whose 'totalising' disourses the student wants to contest. The irony is that she needs to write within them in order to contest them.

The Mutating Visibility and Invisibility of Language

A major problem in the issues I have been discussing is institutional discourse around language. As shown in my demonstration of the historical construction of rhetorical norms for academic literacy, language is ideally invisible. It only becomes visible when it is a problem, as in the above student's case. However, because this visibility should not actually be there, and because when it is there, it is associated also with cognitive deficiency, there is a tendency not to draw attention to it. This is particularly the case, I suspect, at PhD level, when the student is obviously intellectually very competent. This situation of cognitive dissonance, as it were, led to the language issue not being dealt with directly. The student's supervisor told her merely that her text needed 'a bit of smoothing'. The student, for her part, valued the fact that her supervisor reacted only to ideas in her thesis and did not dwell on language issues. She also told me that she did not like what she referred to as the 'administrative' process of editing her work. She opposes this to the creative side of writing, which she does value. Indeed, her writing can be very melodic. Again, I would say that poetic phrasing such as in the following sentence would stand out more, if it was not followed by grammatical and lexical inaccuracies.

> Within an abundance of seductive ideology and promise, postcolonial subject seemly are not capable of the expression action and making themselves for own constitutive life,

One other aspect of the mutating visibility/invisibility dynamic around language is the fact that when language use is good, it is not remarked upon. What makes a good thesis is not the writing, but the thinking. This leads to a kind of 'treading on eggshells' around language which does not always help the students. There is a danger of patronising rather than offering the student opportunities of transculturation, if emphasis is not put on achieving the kind of language proficiency that will enable the manipulation of the representational resources of English for their own ends.

Arguably, the Korean PhD student should simply be given the services of an editor, and this might be alright, if she wanted the PhD for instrumental purposes only and then wanted to return to working in her first language. However, this is unlikely with those students who want to work in the academic world, where publishing in English is frequently a necessity. Flowerdew (2000) describes how a Chinese academic was helped extensively by the editing processes of a specific journal to gain publication. However, he also mentioned how the academic had not 'initially put a high value on the rhetorical dimension of his work' (p. 147) but that now he 'will be more focussed and more concentrated on the style rather than a lot of the content' (p. 143).

In my student's case, I feel that getting to grips with grammar and lexis in English will be as empowering for her as an academic as getting the PhD. I do not wish to fetishise grammar, nor to put the clock back to a concern with structure for its own sake, but to assert the independence, and opportunities for interpolation into world knowledge, that come from a high degree of language proficiency in the currently dominant global language, English.

Acknowledgements

I would like to thank Soyang Park for the abstract in Korean, and for allowing me to record our consultation sessions on her PhD.

Correspondence

Any correspondence should be directed to Joan Turner, Goldsmiths College, Language Unit, University of London, New Cross, London, SE14 6NW, UK (j.turner@gold.ac.uk).

References

Ashcroft, B. (2001) *Post-colonial Transformation* London and New York: Routledge.
Bazerman, C. (1988) *Shaping Written Knowledge*. Madison: University of Wisconsin Press.
Code, L. (1995) *Rhetorical Spaces*. London, Routledge.
Cottingham, J. (1988) *The Rationalists*. Oxford: Oxford University Press.
Delpit, L. (1998) The politics of teaching literate discourse. In V. Zamel and R. Spack (eds) *Negotiating Academic Literacies. Teaching and Learning across Languages and Cultures* (pp. 207–218). Mahwah, NJ: Lawrence Erlbaum.
Flowerdew, J. (2000) Discourse community, legitimate peripheral participation, and the non-native English-speaking scholar. *TESOL Quarterly* 34 (1) 127–150.
Foucault, M. (1970) *The Order of Things: An Archaeology of the Human Sciences*. New York: Random House.
Foucault, M. (1973) *The Birth of the Clinic*. London: Tavistock.
Foucault, M. (1977) *Discipline and Punish: The Birth of the Prison* (tran. A.M. Sheridan Smith). New York: Pantheon.
Giroux, H. (1992) *Border Crossings. Cultural Workers and the Politics of Education*. New York and London: Routledge.
Gonzalez, A. (1987) Poetic imperialism or indigenous creativity? Philippine literature in English. In L. Smith (ed.) *Discourse Across Cultures* (pp. 125–140). London: Macmillan.
Hall, S. (1992) The West and the rest: Discourse and power. In S. Hall and B. Gieben (eds) *Formations of Modernity*. Polity Press in Association with the Open University.
Hall, S. (1996a) Cultural Identity and Diaspora. In Padmini Mongia (ed.) *Contemporary Postcolonial Theory. A Reader*. London: Arnold.

Hall, S.(1996b) When was the post-colonial'? Thinking at the Limit. In Iain Chambers and Lidia Curti (eds) *The Post-colonial Question. Common Skies,Divided Horizons.* London and New York: Routledge.

Harris, R. and Taylor, T. (1989) *Landmarks in Linguistic Thought. The Western Tradition from Socrates to Saussure.* London and New York: Routledge.

Ivanič, R. (1998) *Writing and Identity. The Discoursal Construction of Identity in Academic Writing.* Amsterdam: John Benjamins.

Kachru, B. (1987) The bilingual's creativity: Discoursal and stylistic strategies in contact literatures. In L. Smith (ed.) *Discourse Across Cultures* (pp. 141–156). London: Macmillan.

Lillis, T. and J. Turner (2001) Student writing in higher education: Contemporary confusion, traditional concerns. *Teaching in Higher Education* 6, 57–68.

Nagel, T. (1986) *A View From Nowhere.* Oxford: Oxford University Press.

Parthasarathy, R. (1987) Tradition and creativity: Stylistic innovations in Raja Rao. In L. Smith (ed.) *Discourse Across Cultures* (pp. 157–165). London: Macmillan.

Pratt, M.L. (1992) *Travel Writing and Transculturation.* London and New York: Routledge.

Reddy, M.J. (1979). The conduit metaphor - a case of conflict in our language about language. In A. Ortony (ed.) *Metaphor and Thought* (pp. 284–324). Cambridge: Cambridge University Press.

Trinh T. Minh-ha in conversation with Annamaria Morelli (1996) The undone interval. In I. Chambers and L. Curti (eds) *The Post-colonial Question. Common Skies, Divided Horizons.* London and New York: Routledge.

Turner, J. (1999) Academic literacy and the discourse of transparency. In C. Jones, J. Turner and B. Street (eds) *Students Writing in the University: Cultural and Epistemological Issues* (pp. 149–160). Amsterdam: John Benjamins.

Venn, C. (2000) *Occidentalism. Modernity and Subjectivity.* London: Sage.

Zamel, V. (1997) Toward a Model of Transculturation *Tesol Quarterly* 31, 341–353.

3 Articulating Contact in the Classroom: Towards a Constitutive Focus in Critical Pedagogy

Keith E. Nainby
Hartnell College, San Jose, California, USA

John T. Warren and Christopher Bollinger
School of Communication Studies, Bowling Green State University, Ohio, USA

In this paper we call into question the ontological assumptions within prominent, foundational critical pedagogy literature – particularly the work of Paulo Freire. We suggest that these ontological assumptions may limit critical educational efforts within multicultural communities, because they tacitly reduce our complex, contested class-room interactions to preparatory or subsidiary events within transformative pedagogy. We contend that ongoing classroom communication can itself become an important locus of transformation, if we approach such communication from the perspective of what John Stewart labels a 'one-world,' rather than a 'two-worlds', ontology.

No ensaio seguinte questionamos princípios ontológicos da literatura predominante e fundamental da pedagogia crítica – em particular na obra de Paulo Freire. Sugerimos que estes princípios ontológicos podem restringir os objectivos de uma educação crítica em comunidades multiculturais, uma vez que reduzem tacitamente as interacções complexas e questionáveis em sala de aula a acontecimentos preparatórios e subsidiários, se tivermos em conta uma pedagogia transformadora. Argumentamos que a comunicação corrente numa sala de aula pode tornar-se numa situação promotora de mudança se a abordarmos numa perspectiva holística, que John Stewart identificou como de mundo único – 'one-world', e não numa perspectiva dicotómica, ou seja de dois mundos – 'two-worlds'.

> In problem-posing education, people develop their power to perceive criti-cally *the way they exist* in the world *with which* and *in which* they find them-selves; they come to see the world not as a static reality, but as a reality in process, in transformation. (Freire, 2001: 64)

> Humans are characteristically understanders, beings whose way-of-being is to understand, to construct sense, significance, meaning, and coherence. And humans accomplish this understanding situated in a *world*. Because *world*, thus understood, is the sphere that humans inhabit, *there can be noth-ing outside of it*. The human world consists of everything that affects us and everything we affect. [. . .] *Thus there cannot be two worlds.* (Stewart, 1995: 108)

One of the greatest challenges facing those of us in the present-day academy is finding ways to educate from, with, and for a multitude of cultural perspectives. This challenge becomes acute within our efforts to educate one another critically – because educational practices grounded in the exploration and transformation of oppressive conditions must necessarily begin with educational authority figures (such as teachers) who have a particular sociopolitical interest in critical education. How can we find ways to teach critically while also actively searching

for ways to call privileged perspectives – including our own teacherly perspectives – into question with students? This concern is not a new one in intercultural
communication research, nor in pedagogical scholarship. But our goal in this
paper is to offer one fresh insight into the conundrum of critical education in a
multicultural society by developing a conceptual bridge between contemporary
communication theory and critical educational practice. We will construct that
bridge through the medium of a four-part discussion of ontology: (1) the ontological assumptions inherent in traditional (i.e. representational, non-constitutive)
approaches to communication; (2) the ways in which extant critical educational
theory and practice reflect important elements of these traditional assumptions;
(3) the alternative ontological position offered by a constitutive approach to
communication; and (4) the importance of this alternative position for critical
educators.

We have chosen the two passages above as epigraphs because they indicate an
important set of shared commitments between Paulo Freire and John Stewart,
two authors whose work is central to, respectively, critical educational research
and constitutive communication theory. Freire (2001), in describing the theoretical assumptions grounding what we now know as critical pedagogy in *Pedagogy
of the Oppressed*, characterises human lives and the social conditions that enfold
our lives as processual. These human conditions are fully constituted in and
through social interaction – and therefore, changeable by social interaction.
Stewart (1995) makes very similar claims in *Language as Articulate Contact: Toward
a Post-Semiotic Philosophy of Communication*, as he outlines the salient features of a
'constitutive' approach to communication. He holds that if we acknowledge that
human social life is fully constituted in and through communication, then we
will develop more coherent ideas not only about communication but also about
related social disciplines – such as, by implication, education.

Despite their common descriptions of socially constituted human experience,
however, Freire and Stewart offer distinctively different viewpoints on communication itself and its relation to material reality. For Freire (2001), the central
issue is the human capacity for recognising that social relations are actively
constituted and thus can change. This reflects his goal of developing a
transformative pedagogy. Freire's (2001) pedagogical model posits a material
world which becomes a site of human interpretation and meaning-creation. The
end for Freire, as his emphasis in the text above suggests, is not an 'accurate'
understanding of the world for its own sake. It is instead a deepened conception
of our relation to, and power over, material conditions. Through such a deepened conception the material world itself, and each of us within it, become more
'fully human' (2001: 28–29).

Stewart (1995), in contrast, emphasises the singularity of the socially-created
world in the passage we cited as an epigraph. He argues that we may limit our
understanding of social life by (often unwittingly) retaining a traditional, 'common sense' model of communication. In such a model, an ontological distinction
is implied between the world of communication itself (the world of talk, text, etc.)
and the world that our communication is 'about'. For Stewart, this ontological
distinction necessarily fosters a series of corollary assumptions. He maintains
that this group of assumptions may not lead us down the most fruitful theoretical
paths when we address questions in social research.

Our concern in this paper is the possibility that these 'two-world' assumptions may affect: (1) our exploration, with students, of the socially constituted nature of oppression; and (2) the pedagogical possibilities we work to create with the goal of transforming oppressive conditions. We will show that Freire's (2001) accounts of oppression and of transformative pedagogy – while consonant in significant ways with Stewart's (1995) ideas about the socially constituted character of human life – also imply a 'two worlds' ontology. Freire is an author whose germinal work on critical education has overwhelmingly influenced us (the three authors) as teachers and scholars; his conception of communication as fundamental to social transformation is the starting point of our analysis. Our goal is not to directly refute his conception of communication and its relationship to oppression, but rather to interrogate that conception for the purpose of showing how new insights into communication theory might meaningfully extend it. Specifically, we believe that contemporary communication theory may help to clarify, for critical educators, an important philosophical tangle within Freire's model: namely, how and why classroom-level pedagogical projects can have immediate, concrete material impact within students' present-day lives. For us, a 'one-world' ontology helps illuminate the complex relationship between in-class meaning-making and material oppression. From this perspective, we contend that identifying certain implicit 'two worlds' dimensions of Freire's pedagogical model, and tracing the potential implications of these dimensions for teachers, is appropriate and productive for two reasons.

First, questioning the validity of Freire's assumptions about communication can help us better understand, and perhaps build upon, his educational approach as it pertains to day-to-day classroom activities. These activities must, according to Freire (2001), begin with dialogue:

> Thus, the dialogical character of education as the practice of freedom does ... begin ... when the [teacher-student] first asks herself or himself *what* she or he will dialogue with the [student-teachers] *about*. And preoccupation with the content of dialogue is really preoccupation with the program content of education. (2001: 74)

Through identifying dialogue, or communication, as the necessary social force enabling transformative education, Freire provides a space for such educational projects to develop regardless of the recalcitrance of the local political *status quo*. In this way transformative education might begin in a rural farming community (as it did for Freire's first students), on a shop floor, in a church – or in a contemporary public school. Thus, the possibility that critical educational programmes might succeed here and now, in our classrooms, directly depends for Freire on our ability to communicatively engage students. This means that continued reflection upon the coherence and effectiveness of communication, as conceived within a critical pedagogy context, is a worthwhile building block as we work to make Freire's ideas relevant today.

Second, we find that scholarly efforts to extend Freire's (2001) conceptual work can tacitly perpetuate a traditional 'two worlds' ontology in their assumptions about communication. This is an important possibility to consider because communication is a central component of the conceptual framework undergirding critical pedagogy. Freire, arguing for a radical reformulation of the traditional teacher–student relationship on ethical grounds, insists 'that one must seek to live *with* others in solidarity. One cannot impose oneself, nor even merely co-exist, with one's students. Solidarity requires true communication' (2001: 57–8). This suggests that a more coherent theory of communication and its constitutive aspects can, in and of itself, clarify the ethical principles underlying Freire's ideas – and thus may be a useful extension of contemporary critical pedagogy scholarship.

In using Stewart's (1995) work we will not only provide a critique of how critical pedagogy may imply and be limited by a two-worlds ontology; we will also propose an alternative model for engaging critical pedagogy, a model that tries to highlight and, subsequently, move beyond these limitations. To do this, we will call upon the work of Ira Shor (1996), a critical pedagogy scholar who – while himself still relying on a two-worlds commitment in his own theorising of transformative education – models an approach to pedagogical research that we find hopeful and potentially transformative. This paper concludes with an explication of one of Shor's (1996) latest works in which he investigates his own pedagogy in the moment of teaching, asking critical questions based on his own immediate and communal classroom experiences.

Two Worlds

Stewart (1995: 6–7) describes traditional views of communication as sharing a common point of departure. This point, he observes, is sometimes explicit in an author's framing of communicative activity, and at other times implicit: namely, that communication involves human beings using one class of things to stand in for another class of things. Stewart explains: 'this basic ontological claim ... holds that there is a difference in kind between the linguistic world, or the world of "signifiers," and some other world, that of "things," "mental experiences," "ideas," "concepts," or some other "signifieds"' (p. 7). Thus, the 'two worlds' inherent in traditional, or representational, views of communication might be loosely characterised as: (1) the 'world we communicate with', the entire set of symbols, sounds, gestures, pictures, and other things we use to communicate, and (2) the 'world we communicate about', all of the various subjects that we are moved to talk about with one another.

Throughout his exploration of traditional approaches, Stewart (1995: 7–13) traces a series of four additional 'commitments' that he believes follow inevitably from the primary commitment to the existence of two distinct worlds. We will not explore each of these here.[1] Instead, we will focus on three interrelated implications we find in a two-worlds ontology – implications that are significant for critical pedagogy. These three implications overlap in many ways with the five commitments identified by Stewart, so we will use his analysis to help explicate our concerns about a two-worlds ontology.

The first ontological implication of representational approaches is that the 'world we communicate with' has a material force and a meaningful presence in our lives only when judged by its correspondence to the 'world we communicate about'. In this view, communication is always a postulate about states of affairs, or potential states of affairs, within the world it represents. Factual statements have material force solely because they are more or less accurate, while counterfactual statements (such as future plans, or lies) have material force solely because their representation of potential states of affairs is more or less persuasive. This characteristic of the representational paradigm is highlighted by Stewart (1995: 8) as he notes, 'the two worlds consist of "physical forms" and "events in other channels" or present "symbols" and "the not-necessarily here and the not-necessarily now"'. Communication is thus reduced to: (1) something that functions entirely within a 'non-physical' channel; and (2) something that is materially meaningful only as a 'symbol,' a stand-in, for matter that is not present in the moment. A two-worlds ontology, in this way, emphasises the ephemerality, the softness, of communication by contrasting it with the hard intractability of the material world, which is always either this-way or that-way, always either here or not-here.

A one-world ontology, in contrast, emphasises the immediacy and the material force of communication itself. Such an ontology does not encourage us to suspend judgement about the immediate impact of, for example, racist, sexist, or heterosexist speech until we can assess the material inequities it may perpetuate or ensure. This would be impossible given that, from a constitutive perspective, communication is the only way we have to assess the impact of transformative efforts. There is no vantage point from which we can make non-communicative judgements about material consequences in our lives. Within a constitutive paradigm even our own 'individual' pain or joy, hunger or satisfaction, are sensible to us because we have learned with others to make sense of them. Thus, a communicative act cannot be any more dependent upon 'the facts' for its material significance than 'the facts' themselves are dependent upon the communicative act. As Stewart (1995: 115) maintains, 'in all our knowledge of ourselves and in all knowledge of the world, we are always already encompassed by the language that is our own'. Our claim is not that any one scholar or teacher who works from two-worlds ontological assumptions would deny the material force of violent speech or some other speech. We hold, rather, that a one-world ontology is more coherent, and admits fewer contradictions, than a two-world ontology – at least when the subject matter involves the immediate and the iterative consequences of social interaction. This subject matter is at the heart of the projects of critical educators and theorists.

A second concern is the framing of communication as a means to some future end. This parallels the view of communication as dependent upon material states of affairs, by similarly suspending judgement or appraisal of communicative action until some later end comes to be. Stewart (1995: 114) refers to this as the 'instrumental' or 'tool' model of communication, cautioning, 'one cannot make instrumental use of the constitutive mode of one's being-in-the-world'. Just as we cannot have some independent access, beyond communication, to facts or their value, we cannot experience needs nor formulate ends independently of communication. As Stewart (1995: 116) notes, we come to understand ourselves, others, and our relationship to the world through social interaction. This is what he means by 'one's being-in-the-world': it is communication that forms the very stuff of our lives, unifying human beings and the world. For this reason communication cannot be a mere means to achieve human world-shaping.

This second implication of a two-worlds ontology is, indeed, contrary to one central commitment of critical education: namely, that *how* we learn about a given problem is at least as important as *what* we learn about it. Freire (2001: 64) articulates this commitment in the passage quoted as an epigraph: 'In problem-posing education, people ... come to see the world ... as a reality in process, in transformation.' Problem-posing education, for Freire, does not involve learning how to most efficiently or effectively accomplish some particular end, through communication or any other purportedly subservient means. This tenet calls for, instead, learning to recognise the human situation – in which we always, in each moment, are co-creating our reality with one another. A one-world ontology, therefore, is more consistent with Freire's overall approach to learning.

The third significant implication of a two-worlds ontology is the creation of a hierarchy of value between the two worlds. This hierarchy is a consequence of the two implications already discussed, as the 'world we communicate with' is reduced to a less-than-material means to some greater, more materially equitable end. Hierarchical structures of knowledge like this one should be especially troubling for critical educators, who are in part concerned with the breaking down of such taken-for-granted hierarchies as teacher/student, expert/novice, and benefactor/needy person. But a further problem with such a hierarchy is that it may direct our attention, as educators or as researchers, towards only one limited group of concerns. If the 'world we communicate about' is even indirectly understood as more meaningful than some other world, then those purportedly less meaningful features of human life – for example, our classroom interactions – may become hidden, overlooked in our work. Stewart (1995: 9) notes this tendency in linguistic scholarship, observing that the two-worlds assumption 'has also highlighted some kinds of parts [of communicative action] and ignored others with as much or more semantic and pragmatic importance'. While we cannot avoid making choices that foreground some questions and background others, a one-world ontology can help us better sustain an interest in the multiple connections among meanings, experiences, and transformative possibilities in our lives.

Freire and Communication

Freire's (2001) characterisation of communication and its relation to human lives and conditions is closely aligned with the constitutive approach advocated by Stewart. However, Freire also, in key passages on communication, retains significant elements of a two-worlds ontological vocabulary. This raises the possibility that contemporary critical pedagogues and scholars might work more effectively from Freire's conceptual foundation if its ontological commitments were explored and clarified. In order to discuss our extension of Freire's work, we first offer his conceptual frame for critical pedagogy.

Freire's (2001) central assumption in *Pedagogy of the Oppressed* is that oppressive conditions are not merely sustained by brute economic or political forces, but more importantly by the totality of our ideas about ourselves, the world, and our collective options. He holds regarding people living in an oppressive society:

> the very structure of their thought has been conditioned by the contradictions of the concrete, existential situation by which they were shaped. Their ideal is to be [women or] men, but for them, to be [women or] men is to be oppressors. This is their model of humanity. (2001: 27)

In this description, social interaction becomes the very mode of our relation to self and world; it is both that which constrains us and that which has the power to help us free ourselves. Thus, Freire conforms here to a constitutive view of communication while articulating a fundamental element of the world-perspective of critical pedagogy.

In *Pedagogy of Hope: Reliving Pedagogy of the Oppressed*, Freire (1994) reconsiders his framework for transformative pedagogy in light of 25 additional years of teaching and learning. He focuses more directly on communication in this text; perhaps his most significant appraisal of it is that 'changing language is part of the process of changing the world. The relationship, language-thought-world, is a dialectical, processual, contradictory relationship' (1994: 67–68). Freire contends here that the very words we choose, as we learn to name our world through pedagogical projects, become sources of creative potential for each of us. This further develops his earlier tenet that 'those who have been denied their primordial right to speak their word must first reclaim this right' (2001: 69).

Freire (2000) reaffirms this constitutive perspective on communication in a later text of reflections on specific pedagogical practices, entitled *Education For a Critical Consciousness*. He remembers, 'our traditional curriculum ... centered on words emptied of the reality they are meant to represent. ... Our verbal culture corresponds to our inadequacy of dialogue, investigation, and research' (2000: 37). In this analysis Freire highlights the ways in which received, state-sponsored, 'banking' models of education depend first and foremost on preserving a static, passive relationship between students' understanding of the world and the 'facts' of the world itself. The problem with traditional pedagogies, from his perspective, is precisely that they fail to acknowledge the world-constituting capacity of human social action.

Yet Freire's articulation of the role of communication also includes terminology consonant with a two-worlds ontology, which offers an opportunity to extend and sharpen his critical focus. He presumes that 'words ... are meant to represent' reality, while tacitly affirming that 'verbal culture corresponds to' a specific mental construct, namely 'inadequacy' (2000: 37). His strong implication here is that students and teachers can and should intervene critically in our lives by, in part, judging communicative acts according to whether they adequately correspond to either our present world or some possible future world. We contend that these ideas – which are products of a two-world ontology – are, as Stewart (1995: 113) insists, 'incommensurable with' the one-world ontology that characterises a constitutive view of communication. From what standpoint might we judge, in a classroom interaction, the correspondence between communication and some other world? Such efforts would necessarily be fraught with contradictions inherent in critical projects within a society steeped in hegemonic discourses and historic oppressions, as Freire himself would acknowledge. Our contention is that moving away from language like 'represent' and 'correspond' can help us to work more effectively towards untangling these contradictions, by foregrounding the simultaneity of speech acts and material effects – and, perhaps, thereby also foregrounding the power we have as human beings to remake the world.

The potential conceptual difficulties of a two-world ontology can be seen in Freire's description of 'the relationship, language-thought-world' (1994: 67). He emphasises the 'dialectical' and 'processual' character of this structure, an emphasis which again conforms with constitutive perspectives. But such a relationship, in its 'contradictory' nature, also has three direct consequences inherent in its structure – consequences that may be not only contradictory but incommensurable as well. These relate to the three objections we raise about two-worlds assumptions: (1) language and world are not immediately present with one another, but are instead mediated by thought. An implication of this is that language may not have an immediate, material presence in our lives. (2) Thought itself – the sum of our sense-making projects – is not an endpoint within this structure. It functions, through its mediating role, as a bridge between the social world (language) and the material world (world). Mental concepts are, in this way, subtly reduced to a 'means' status, parallel to the reduction of communicative acts in general to 'means' within a two-worlds ontology. (3) Even within a dialectically nuanced three-part structure, if 'language-thought-world' stand in a linear relation to one another then hierarchies of value will be likely to develop. Such a development would stem from the lack of an immediate connection between language and world, as well as the dependence of thought on its language-world-mediating role.

We trace the impulse to postulate thought as a mediator between social life and material life to the persistence of a dualistic ontology, in which human inner experience is held to be utterly unlike (and, typically, superior to) the brute physical realm. Such assumptions permeate our cultural milieu; they are tacitly interwoven into much of our discourse about, in particular, how we should relate to the world socioeconomically, as consumers of resources. For this reason, we hold that working to challenge a dualism-based outlook on future human relationships is a central objective for critical educators. Working from Freire's three-part linear model may make it more difficult for students and teachers to conceptualise the depth and complexity of our connection to one another – a connection that is both material and social at once. We might instead work from a model such as concentric clouds, in which the communicative, conceptual, and material dimensions of human life are posited as distinct yet overlapping, without a built-in linear, dependent, or hierarchical relationship to one another. We maintain that a deep, enduring harmony among human living conditions, human sociality, and human projects is a vital component of critical pedagogy. Thus, we are interested in working towards a respecification of the character of communication within critical pedagogy, in terms that foreground the singularity – rather than the duality – of dimensions of human life. In the following section we offer some preliminary ideas on such a project.

Towards a Constitutive Focus in Critical Pedagogy

One core idea in Freire's *Pedagogy of the Oppressed* is that such a pedagogy can be meaningfully conceptualised as two distinct stages (2001: 36). We contend that these distinct stages are a direct consequence of a two-worlds ontology. For Freire, oppressive conditions are tangled up amid a self-perpetuating nexus of material suffering and passive meaning-acceptance – not hopelessly so, but sufficiently tangled that the first stage is necessary. In this stage, again, 'the oppressed unveil the world of oppression and through the praxis commit themselves to its transformation' (2001: 36). Freire's primary concern here is not merely that the oppressed do not recognise or have recourse to their own world-constituting powers; it is, in the first stage, that this situation prevents the oppressed from transforming reality. This is why we need two pedagogical stages in Freire's model: because initially, in an oppressive society, there is a lack of correspondence between what we understand about 'reality' (its permanence, its naturalness, our own passivity in relation to it) and what is actually true about this same reality (its socially-sustained character, our own world-constituting capacities, and so on).

If we endeavour to move away from the assumptions and vocabulary of a two-worlds ontology, however, then we may no longer see oppression as a lack of correspondence between meaning and reality. One way we might do this is by emphasising day-to-day speech acts as an important subject matter of both our scholarly and our pedagogical work. If we do so we can reframe oppression as, in Stewart's (1995: 24) terms, an incoherence, a lack of plausibility in our immediate lives rather than an inadequate representational correspondence. Stewart maintains, 'to be human is to engage in the life processes of coming to an understanding (everyday coping). ... Even when engaged in intractable conflict, humans are collaboratively constructing or negotiating their worlds' (p. 112). This claim about what it means to be human is consonant with Freire's (2001) on one level, because it centres on our world-constituting powers. Yet, it also offers an important extension of the critical pedagogy framework by suggesting that, even in oppressive conditions, we are each always already world-constituting beings.

This does not mean that oppressive conditions can simply be 're-constituted' away, however. A one-world ontology highlights the unity of social meaning and social reality; neither meaning nor reality is more significant nor more easily amenable to the transformation Freire demands. Stewart (1995: 117–118) writes, 'To say we inherit and inhabit the world is to say in part that we are constrained by it to at least as great a degree as we constrain it. The "it" that constrains us and that we constrain, however, is *world* not "reality" or "brute data".' This clarification is crucial in contemporary critical pedagogy scholarship because it implies a necessary balance among scholars' attention to material conditions, social forces, and (in Stewart's words) everyday coping. One tendency in prominent critical pedagogy texts is an overemphasis either on the material (McLaren, 1994, 1997, 2000) or the social (Giroux, 1997, 2000, 2001) at the expense of everyday human life; such tendencies suggest that alternatives might lie in the more mundane site of classroom interactions.

In a one-world ontology, human life is presumptively constitutive, day-to-day. From this perspective each of us is living through, in a multiplicity of ways, our world-constituting abilities. There is, without question, a need to draw attention to these in educational projects and to work together, as teacher-students and student-teachers, to rethink how and why we constitute the world as we do. But the 'unveiling' and the 're-creating' processes are one and the same in a one-world ontology. This is a potentially energising respecification of critical pedagogical theory, in our estimation, because a one-world ontology foregrounds the immediate impact, on an everyday classroom level, of our active world-constituting activities. The implication that critical pedagogical projects are merely a means to a better end, simply a first stage that mediates between today's material suffering and tomorrow's eventual liberation, falls away within a one-world ontology.

Freire cautions future critical pedagogues: 'the educator needs to know that his or her "here" and "now" are almost always the educands' "there" and "then"' (1994: 58). This caution points to one daunting challenge we have faced as educators: the difficulty of making problem-posing education seem relevant to university students whose educational experiences have, in many cases, rewarded them only for focusing on short-term scholastic, economic, and social benefits while punishing any broader efforts they have undertaken to make sense of their lives through schooling. Struggling to find, with students, the ways that everyday communication actively constitutes, structures, and constrains our world can help teachers cut through the heart of the 'what's in it for me?' argument by highlighting the immediate power of communication, power that may be both oppressive and liberating depending on local contexts. This raises the stakes, for many students are not accustomed to working against oppressive structures while in class; but it can help to make critical educational projects come to life, lifting Freire off the page and into the classroom. Thus, a theoretical approach that encourages us to focus on the constitutive forces operating in the 'here' and 'now' is in the spirit – if not at all times the 'ontological letter' – of Freire's vision. Such an approach can be a valuable component of a meaningful critical pedagogy.

Our detailing of Freire (1994, 2000, 2001) and Stewart (1995) begs the question: what hope exists for creating a classroom context that begins to disrupt the unproductive (and confining) split between the purportedly distinct worlds of meaning and reality? We begin any discussion of change based in Stewart's philosophy by noting that, as members of a community entrenched in a representational paradigm, it is difficult to imagine our way out of the box we have created – the inconsistencies we identify in Freire's work above also pervade everyday discourse, in such a way that finding new approaches are, to say the least, a challenge. That said, we find the possibility of working towards a one-world paradigm vital and the potential rewards significant. The two-worlds ontology implicit in critical pedagogy constrains and conditions our classroom practices such that, unless we seek change, we risk reconstituting the very oppressions we seek to eliminate.

Thus, we aim to undermine the two-worlds divide, arguing that the artificial 'meaning' representing 'reality' only works to reduce efforts at political and social change, never truly working at the site of how such 'realities' are (re)made. By affirming such divisions, we only reproduce problematic binaries already filtered through our educational and social lives. Consider the example of the theory/practice divide. This division is contrary to the foundational tenets of Freire's model – yet one might chart out how prominent critical education literature at times reproduces this binary. Theory, or the world of meaning-making, serves to guide or direct our practice, or our realities in the classroom. McLaren and Giroux then become only representations, only figures that stand in for or represent our lives, experiences, and practices in the classroom. Since McLaren and Giroux rarely talk through their own classroom experiences, one might see their work only as guides that provide access to how we, the practitioners in the classroom, should work. This potential hierarchy does not serve our classrooms or our students. Further, the separation and lack of correspondence between the reality of our classrooms and how we understand the active, communicative constitution of those classroom spaces divorces students themselves from the process of education. The students become a by-product, a secondary thought. This reproduces the very power structure that Freire (2001) began to critique in his critical pedagogy project – he sought to undermine such top-down pedagogies, not rebuild them in a different image.

Shor's Struggles: Towards a 'One-World' Classroom

For the reasons outlined in this paper, we seek a one-world classroom – a classroom that begins from and theorises through interaction. To do so, we turn to Ira Shor's (1996) *When Students Have Power: Negotiating Authority in a Critical Pedagogy*. We turn to this book not because Shor completely shakes off the shackles of two-world ontology, but rather because we see some potential in his process. In Shor's book, he traces his own work in a classroom context and asks how his efforts at creating critical pedagogy in the classroom actually work: 'in this story about a Dewey-Freire model of democratic power relation, I will try to make my writing itself an experiment about the experiment. That is, I want this personal report to cross genres' (1996: xi). Shor has long been a proponent of foregrounding, in his writing, his own classrooms practices, having spent most of his research career charting out what critical education looks like within the site of the classroom.[2] Shor articulates his specific goal in this book:

> I will also be in dialogue with myself, hoping to be self-critical, interrogating my own position while trying to represent fairly and to present extensively the positions of the students (through examples of their own production and expressions). (pp. xi–xii)

Shor's book, then, is a documentary of his own working of critical pedagogy in the classroom.

In certain ways, this book reproduces the two-worlds assumptions this paper seeks to critique – Shor (1996) begins with a set of assumptions and ideals of what it means to create a libratory classroom prior to entering the classroom. As an educator and researcher in critical pedagogy, Shor (like many of us) approaches the classroom knowing the liberatory and transformative educational literature. This approach is evident early on in the book as he makes claims about his classroom and his assumptions of his students:

> But, even though I think of [my students] as 'working-class,' they generally don't think of themselves in those terms, which is a large gap between our understandings. This is a grand cultural canyon separating us–how I have learned to see and name them, myself, and our teacherly learning relationship versus how they have learned to see themselves, the teacher, and what it means to be a student who works for a living. 'Class' is an invisible identity in American life, denied and dismissed. (p. 8)

Here, we see that even though Shor may begin with different assumptions and understandings from those of his students, he continues to push his own vision of their identity. The shift to 'class is invisible' within Shor's argument is a marking of his own definitional authority – as one reads this text, one tends to see these students as victims of class, unknowingly part of an oppressed group without the knowledge of their own positions.

However, these assumptions soon bump against the wills of the students who have different ideas about the nature of education and their roles within the classroom. Here, we see the result of a two-worlds ontology – the representational paradigm fails to account for the complexity of lived experiences. In a sense the initial failure of this classroom context is precisely the belief in the two-worlds model to which Freire, perhaps inadvertently, subscribes. Remember, Freire (2001) discusses the necessity of a two-tier critical pedagogy project, seeing the social and charting out a new way of being, and actualising the transformed vision in everyday life. There, the emphasis is on systemic meanings rather than minute everyday communicative acts. This is reflected in Shor's (1996) initial approach in his own classroom, in which the systemic (read, his critical pedagogical vision and his own vision of liberation) takes precedence over the immediate needs of the classroom. This is evident in the early parts of the book as he discusses 'the Siberian Syndrome', a condition of sitting in the back of the room as if 'aggressively in exile' (p. 12).

Shor's book, and his struggles in implementing a critical pedagogy in that space, are in many ways a perfect documentation of how and why the two-world ontology in critical pedagogy fails. By approaching the students (i.e. the reality and everydayness of this classroom experience) through a prior, definitive set of assumptions (theoretical/philosophical tenets that describe a systemic, relational correspondence), the students bucked and resisted the efforts Shor made. In perhaps the first direct notation of resistance, Shor tells about students' reactions to this writing prompt: 'Why are you taking this class?' What he finds is that many are taking this class as a credit – a way to fulfil the institution's requirements for a degree. This prompts Shor (1996: 31) to reflect on the power of even offering courses, noting that students 'have no institutional power to propose their own courses'. This conflict allows Shor early on to see how attempts to negotiate power and create more meaningful educational experiences create the very possibility for resistance. Shor's students are not engaged in a democratic process – they are not 'citizens', not collaborators in this process (p. 31).

The critique of Shor's (1996) initial attempts aside, we do find much of this book exciting and potentially useful as a model for a constitutive critical pedagogy. Shor, in an effort to problem solve in his classroom (that is, to ask 'why isn't this working?'), creates an 'after-class group' that meets with him to talk through the class. In these sessions, students negotiate with Shor, both demanding accountability for his teaching choices as well as advocating changes in the course plan. Shor finds that, if he wants students to participate and, in Freirean (2001) terms, become student-teachers in this context, he must redirect his preconceived notions of classroom goals and efforts towards the student's own desires. His concluding thoughts on 'what worked and didn't work' in his classroom serves as a sounding board from which he can begin to re-theorise critical pedagogy's future.

Given Shor's (1996) struggles, we find some hope in the method of this book. That is, what this book (and Shor's work in general) foregrounds is the immediate context of teaching and learning. It is this focus that creates contexts for rethinking communication in critical pedagogy research, for Shor builds up his key themes in the book through his classroom interactions. The ultimate message in this book is not that prescriptive, top-down solutions just need actualising in the classroom. Rather, Shor's book stands as a living example of what happens in the moment – what kind of pedagogy can be generated in interaction and what kind of change such an engagement can foster. It is a constitutive theorising of education in context, fulfilling the Freirean goals of beginning in the site and demanding that the goals and ideas of the local community dictate the educational process. Shor's (1996) book can be read, if one puts it in dialogue with Stewart (1995), as a move towards the everyday, towards the active making of reality *through* the interactive meaning-making process of communication. Communication, in this text, shifts from a tool used to help students see 'real' material inequalities (McLaren) or the large-scale social hegemony instituted in education (Giroux), to communication as an interactive, day-to-day, knowledge-producing medium. In Shor's book, we see communication as the only world – these students are making and remaking knowledge in dialogue, in the here and now of educational activity.

Conclusion

Our central endeavours in this paper have been to outline the ontological differences between existing critical pedagogy scholarship and Stewart's work in communication theory, and to show that these differences make a difference as we enter the classroom with critical agendas. Perhaps the most important difference we have addressed, in terms of its impact on contemporary education, is the link between a two-worlds ontology and a two-stage critical pedagogy. From the standpoint of a two-worlds ontology, students can learn to identify oppression in their lives primarily by noticing that words and other public forms of communication do not adequately correspond to the existing world; for example, 'student representatives' within a local community (i.e. the students elected or otherwise chosen to ensure a voice for students in institutional proceedings) may be seen, upon critical reflection in the first stage, to do everything other than represent the needs of students. This recognition prepares students to enter the second stage, in which they can work to transform such conditions. But from the standpoint of a one-world ontology, students might come to understand that 'student representatives' do, in fact, represent 'students' as they are frequently positioned within institutional settings: namely, passive recipients of administrative or governmental dicta. Such an approach might encourage students to recognise that the relationship between communication and material conditions is ongoing, is sustained by the choices they make in every moment, and can thus begin to be changed even in the next moment. While such beginnings may be small, they are beginnings nonetheless – and not merely preparatory work oriented towards a second stage of being. We believe that giving students and teachers an ontological vocabulary that lends their classroom activities a sense of immediacy is an important component of an empowering education in our present-day context – a context rife with apathy and resignation from officials, parents and educators that is transferred too often to students, and that is too often leavened only by so-called 'accountability' measures.

We end this paper with an appeal to scholars and educators in the fields of communication studies and education to find new ways to dialogue. Communication theory has much to offer the field of education, just as the work in education continues to push and define the importance of the work in finding new ways of understanding the nature of our communicative world. Indeed, it is in the moment of articulate contact – in the interactions between us – that we strive to find hope and chart out more equitable social relations. We, like Freire, desire social relationships that inflict less violence and it is within his tradition that we offer this analysis. For we believe that the important work of critical pedagogy, if it is to be successful, relies on seeing how power is actively reconstituted through our communication. It is through recognising, theorising, and fully accounting for our constitutive capacities that we can find new ways of imagining the future, new ways of transforming our classrooms into sites of libratory practice.

Acknowledgements

We wish to thank Alison Phipps and Laura Lengel, who through their efforts encouraged the writing of this paper, and Lenore Langsdorf for her ongoing care and support.

Correspondence

Any correspondence should be directed to Keith E. Nainby, Hartnell College, 262 Truckee Ln, San Jose, California 95136, USA (knainby@yahoo.com).

Notes

1. Stewart (1995) claims that, as a result of the commitment to a two-worlds philosophy of communication, that four other commitments follow. First, he believes that communication becomes atomistic; that is, rather than being viewed as a holistic meaning-making process, communication is understood as a collection of smaller parts (symbols, signs, or other units of meaning) that, only when put together, create a representation of the material world. Second, a traditional model of communication relies on a representational system – that is, communication, which lacks materiality, stands in for or represents the 'real world' of our material things. Third, representational models of communication consider communication a closed system–its component parts meaningful only in relation to one another. Finally, a representational view reduces communication to a mere tool or cultural artefact that humans use in order to navigate our material worlds. In this sense, communication is not a primary mode of being, but a tool we use to move through our material worlds. Each of these assumptions is, in some way, available as a potential reading in critical pedagogy literature because each follow from a belief in a two-world ontology. See Stewart (1995: 6–9) for more explicit details on the five commitments that make more semiotic or representational models of communication problematic.
2. See Shor's (1992, 1980) other work as specific examples of his documented efforts with students in the context of their own classrooms.

References

Freire, P. (1994) *Pedagogy of Hope: Reliving Pedagogy of the Oppressed* (ed. and trans M. Bergman Ramos). New York: Continuum.
Freire, P. (2000) *Education For a Critical Consciousness* (ed. and trans M. Bergman Ramos). New York: Continuum.
Freire, P. (2001) *Pedagogy of the Oppressed: 30th Anniversary Edition* (ed. and trans M. Bergman Ramos). New York: Continuum.

Giroux, H.A. (1997) *Pedagogy and the Politics of Hope: Theory, Culture, and Schooling*. Boulder CO: Westview.

Giroux, H.A. (2000) *Impure Acts: The Practical Politics of Cultural Studies*. New York: Routledge.

Giroux, H.A. (2001). *The Mouse that Roared*. Lanham, MD: Rowman and Littlefield.

McLaren, P. (1994) *Life in Schools: An Introduction to Critical Pedagogy in the Foundations of Education* (2nd edn). White Plains, NY: Longman.

McLaren, P. (1997) *Revolutionary Multiculturalism: Pedagogies of Dissent for the New Millennium*. Boulder, CO: Westview.

McLaren, P. (2000) *Che Guevara, Paulo Freire, and the Pedagogy of Revolution*. Lanham, MD: Rowman and Littlefield.

Shor, I. (1980) *Critical Teaching and Everyday Life*. Chicago: University of Chicago Press.

Shor, I. (1992) *Empowering Education: Critical Teaching for Social Change*. Chicago: University of Chicago Press.

Shor, I. (1996) *When Students have Power: Negotiating Authority in a Critical Pedagogy*. Chicago: University of Chicago Press.

Stewart, J. (1995) *Language as Articulate Contact: Toward a Post-Semiotic Philosophy of Communication*. Albany: SUNY.

4 Listen to the Voices of Foreign Language Student Teachers: Implications for Foreign Language Educators

Rosario Diaz-Greenberg
California State University San Marcos, USA

Ann Nevin
Arizona State University West, Phoenix, USA

The purpose of this paper is to better understand how critical pedagogy and multicultural education can help meet the challenges that world language teachers experience in the teaching of culture. The authors believe that eliciting and understanding the voices of foreign language student teachers is essential to help them learn to mediate their own learning and prepare to teach a multiculturally diverse population in 21st century classrooms. Foreign-language professors may be encouraged to respect and facilitate the struggles involved in acquiring and teaching other languages by incorporating principles of critical pedagogy and techniques from multicultural education.

El propósito de este artículo es entender mejor cómo la Pedagogía Crítica y la Educación Multicultural pueden ayudar a superar las dificultades que los maestros de idiomas experimentan en la enseñanza de la cultura.
Los autores creen que es imprescindible el pedir la opinión de los profesores de idiomas extranjeros a la vez que entender sus cuestionamientos. Escucharlos servirá para ayudarles a guiar su propio aprendizaje de tal manera que puedan prepararse para enseñar a la población multicultural y diversa de las aulas del siglo 21. La incorporación de principios de la Pedagogía Crítica y de técnicas de la Educación Multicultural puede incentivar a los profesores universitarios de idiomas extranjeros a respetar y sobrellevar las dificultades que se enfrentan al aprender y enseñar otros idiomas.

Keywords: critical pedagogy, multicultural education, foreign language instruction, cultural diversity

The purpose of this paper is to explore through student teachers' reflections some of the factors that influence the teaching of culture in the foreign language high school classroom in the United States and what happens when their voices emerge. It also helped to uncover how students perceive their own cultural and linguistic reality within the classroom, and to explore some alternatives that can promote the emergence and legitimatisation of voice in the educational system. This paper aimed to listen to the silent voices of students and learn from them. As Nieto (1994) pointed out, listening to students' voices is the beginning of a reform process to change school policies and practices. Unfortunately, most studies do not include the students' perceptions of the problems, thus creating a gap: 'Students perspectives are ... missing in discussions concerning strategies for confronting educational problems. ... [Their] voices are rarely heard in the debates about school failure and success. ... The perspectives of students from disempowered and dominated communities are ... invisible' (p. 396).

The absence of verbal interaction between teachers and students in the American classroom has been carefully scrutinised by Goodlad (1984), Silberman

(1970) and Sizer (1997), among others. In an appalling manner, teacher-talk dominates 70% of the instructional time spent in verbal interaction. Most of it emanates from teacher to students, and does not allow student-talk to occur (Sirotnik, 1981). Goodlad (1984) observed that, on an average, approximately 75% of class time was spent on instruction. Of that time, 70% flowed as 'talk' from teacher to students. In 1984 Sizer reported that within the American classroom, 'there is little opportunity for sustained conversation between student and teacher. The mode is a one-sentence or two-sentence exchange ... Dialogue is strikingly absent.' Nowhere is this situation more evident than the foreign language classroom where communication skills had never been stressed until the 1990s, as shown in the following brief history of foreign-language teaching in the United States.

In the United States, the history of foreign-language teaching and the preparation of foreign language instructors points to the fact that for decades, grammar and translation approaches were favoured over a communications approach. As a result, students were expected to be 'able to read, write and translate in the foreign language rather than be able to speak it' (ACTFL, 2002: 6). Entire generations were schooled in this manner with the result that individuals were excellent readers, writers and translators but were not able to communicate orally in the target language. It was not until the late 1950s that the necessity of having individuals who would not only be literate but who were also able to speak and had some knowledge of the target culture became a priority. In 1999 the National Standards in Foreign Language Project stated, 'The United States must educate students who are equipped linguistically and culturally to communicate in a pluralistic American society and abroad' (p. 7). Teachers as well as their professors in teacher education programmes must be prepared to meet the demands that ethnically and linguistically diverse populations bring to the classroom.

However, as Pufahl *et al.*, (2000) state in a report prepared for the US Department of Education's Comparative Information on Improving Education Practice, 'During the last two decades, there have been numerous reports and articles decrying the mediocrity of our students' foreign language skills and calling for improved language education.' Attempts were made to improve world language instruction and the preparation of teachers of foreign language. A group of nine foreign language associations worked collaboratively to create the Standards for Foreign Language Learning in the 21st Century (1999).

Meanwhile, as summarised by Axelrod and Bigelow (1962), the National Defense Education Act (NDEA) of 1958 established intensive programmes where individuals would not only become proficient in the language, but also versed in the culture of the target population. As a result, many activities that supported the teaching of foreign language were funded under Title VI of the 1965 Higher Education Act. Furthermore, Dutcher (1996) explains that the National Security Education Act (1992) was launched in order to promote the development of specialists in languages that were less commonly studied. The premise underlying this approach was the development of a capacity to respond in languages and areas of the world which may present a security threat to the United States.

Phillips and Draper (1999) illustrated a paradigmatic change in the teaching of languages. The Five C's – Communication, Cultures, Connections, Comparisons and Communities – were imaged as interlocking circles to signify the importance of including each and every one of them in a systematic approach at all levels of language instruction. As such, the establishment of the standards marked a turning point in the teaching of languages. Language teachers were expected to shift gears and begin looking at culture as an essential element in their language instruction. In the same manner, professors in charge of preparing new foreign language teachers were expected to make sure that their teacher candidates learned to teach culture by incorporating multicultural teaching methods in their university classrooms. In 2002 such attempts were incorporated in the programme standards for the preparation of foreign-language teachers. In fact, two of the five standards deal with the issue of culture directly (Standards 2 and 4).

In contrast, according to Lange (1999), some foreign language teachers merely help students demonstrate an understanding of the practices, products, and perspectives of the culture being studied, as well as show an understanding of the concept of culture through comparisons of the culture studied to their own. This approach can limit the definition of culture, trivialises the complex nature of all cultures, and reduces instructional content to what multiculturalists refer to as the Four Fs approach: Food, Fashion, Festivals and Folklore (Banks, 2002; Sleeter & Grant, 2002) Furthermore, by asking students to compare other cultures with their own, the Four Fs approach assumes that the students will recognise their own stereotypes, put them aside, and then discern that their culture is not superior but only different from the culture of the target language. This is a difficult task for students in the United States because, as Pufahl *et al.*, (2000: 11) state in their report prepared for the US Department of Education's Comparative Information on Improving Education Practice, 'All too often U.S. parents and educators feel that they do not have anything to learn from other countries and must only look to other examples within our own country'.

The issue can be described as follows: when teaching foreign languages, the teacher's perspective of 'culture' determines the learners' first impressions of the culture being studied. If the teacher has a Five Cs approach, the learners may acquire a more complex understanding of the people who speak the language they are studying. In comparison, with teachers whose understanding of the culture is more of the Four Fs variety, learners may acquire a more superficial understanding of the culture in which the language is spoken.

The purpose of the study reported in this paper is to determine to what extent foreign language teacher candidates might understand the distinction between the Five Cs approach and the Four Fs approach. The principles of critical pedagogy, multicultural education and world language education formed the theoretical framework for a dialogic retrospection of the teacher candidates. Within critical pedagogy, education can be seen as a liberatory learning process in which all individuals, regardless of class, race, gender, language of origin, and ethnicity, become conscious of their ability to promote effective change for the betterment of society. Critical pedagogy helps teacher candidates to deconstruct preconceived notions that only benefit the dominant minority. The result, hopefully, is a more liberatory approach that promotes the transformation of the self, a dialogic retrospection process is one way to become aware of the transformation. Reflection plays an essential role in this process, since it provides an opportunity to look back and connect previous experiences to present realities and construct new meaning.

The concept of *conscientization* (Freire, 1998) refers to the development of an awareness of one's self in the world, and no one person can be rejected from experiencing this type of awareness. Through the process of a dialogical interaction (using empowering language, providing supports for communication), the individual can create a mental awareness of one point of view and its opposite (i.e. a *dialectic*). This can lead to the experience of *praxis*, or a cycle of action-reflection-new action such as a self-awareness that can transform the individual's experience of the world. The art of reflection can be seen as the process of looking back. Maturana and Varela (1992: 24) stated, 'the process of knowing how we know ... an act of turning back upon ourselves ... the only chance we have to discover our blindness and to recognize that the certainties and knowledge of others are, respectively, as overwhelming and tenuous as our own.' Reflection is an active process that provides an opportunity to look at past experiences and relate them to future action. It creates a space for discovering new realms within the self and unveiling previously unknown connections that exist between an individual's life in relationship to the lives of others. Educators sometimes believe that they are not able to provide the class time for reflection owing to the need to complete predetermined syllabi and objectives. Student teachers as well as their pupils may inadvertently be shortchanged in this process since they cannot take the initiative and propose that they need time to step back before going on to the next item.

In a series of studies where we applied the principles of critical pedagogy (Freire, 1970) and inclusive education (Villa & Thousand, 1995), we reported that listening to the voices of students with disabilities was an important component of *praxis* (Diaz-Greenberg *et al.*, 2000; Thousand *et al.*,1999). Similarly, when foreign language teachers can listen to the voices of their students, and when teacher education professors can listen to their student teachers, we believe that principles of critical pedagogy and multicultural education might help both teachers and their professors of teacher education become more responsive and culturally aware. How can teacher education professors benefit from an understanding of the contributions of critical pedagogists and multicultural educators who study the processes of conscientisation (a concept from critical pedagogy) and culturally sensitive instructional practices (a concept from multicultural education)? To address this overarching question, we posed the following interview questions to foreign language student teachers. These questions were selected because in addressing them, we believed that they would discover both their conscious and their unconscious beliefs about the nature of their understanding of culture when teaching foreign languages.

(1) How is the concept of culture approached in the textbook you are using during your student teaching?
(2) How is the textbook concept of culture similar or different to what you have learned in the teacher education program, or how concepts of culture are taught in the language classroom?

Method

The researchers interviewed foreign language student teachers who agreed to speak about their schooling experiences in a teacher preparation programme and their student teaching. The resulting essays were analysed for generative themes across all participants for each question. Heaney (1995) stated that generative themes that emerge from the complex experiences of a person's life are charged with political significance and are likely to generate considerable discussion and analysis. From the verbatim transcripts of the interviews, the researchers identified comments that could be correlated with tasks of the foreign language professor as well as concepts associated with the two major approaches to teaching culture in the foreign language classroom.

The first step in the analysis of the data encompassed reading all the dialogues to gain a general understanding of students' perspectives on different issues. A second reading involved looking for key words that would illuminate different topics of concern. Key terms were highlighted to colour-code them. The essays were separated according to key terms. Each essay was reassessed to identify the most significant statements. Reflection and interpretation were necessary to uncover the meaning implied in each identified statement and to determine major themes (Wolcott, 1990).

Colour-coding (Seidman, 1991) the statements according to themes proved helpful to prepare for the next step in the analysis. The major statements of formulated meanings were organised into clusters in terms of themes. The major themes were compared with the original text in order to check for accuracy and comprehension. The revised clusters were then synthesised. The researchers carefully re-read the essays, analysed the themes in terms of the two questions, then organised the themes in the same order as the research questions, and summarised the results.

Who are the interviewees?

The interviewees comprised a convenience sample of graduate students who were completing their last semester in the teacher preparation programme. All had obtained a degree in foreign languages from a four-year university course and had already taken prerequisite courses on education for cultural diversity. Also, they had successfully completed a 15-week class where they learned core concepts about reflective teaching. They were well versed in the concepts of critical pedagogy that they had studied for two semesters in their previous classes for K-12 certification as bilingual, cultural and linguistic educators.

Meet Bridget: 'I think I was about six years old when I first wanted to be a teacher. I remember I used to love to play school with my friends. But I always got mad because my friend was older than me and she never let me be the teacher. I always wanted to play the teacher. My mom has told me that she remembers that I used to answer "teacher" when people would ask me what I wanted to be when I grew up. As I got older I think I forgot that I wanted to be a teacher and thought about doing other things. But when I was in high school, and I had some really great teachers, I contemplated once again being a teacher. But I still wasn't one hundred percent sure. Then while doing my undergraduate work, I had the opportunity to study in Spain. It was while I was there that I made the decision to be a teacher. I think I was about nineteen years old at the time. I came home, declared Spanish as my major, and took all the necessary prerequisite courses, and now here I am. I can't remember exactly what it was that made me decide for sure that I wanted to be a teacher, but something sort of clicked in my head while I was in Spain and I just *knew* that I wanted to pursue a career in teaching. I can't remember who my heroes and heroines were at the time, or really what was going on in the world. I do know that when I was six my parents got a divorce and we moved to California, but I can't say that that influenced me at all in my decision.'

Meet Laura: Laura, despite a successful Hollywood career, decided to become a teacher after returning home to the Midwest to visit an ailing mother. She explained, 'I had a professional job as a translator for a well-known marketing firm. I was young and making great money but somehow left the office everyday completely depressed and unfulfilled with my life. I decided that I would take the risk and give the movie making business a try since it was always my dream to work in feature films. Soon after I became an Assistant Director and was working full-time (sometimes as many as 20 hours a day). I loved what I did though my life was my job. It was glamorous but at the same time hard work and long crazy hours. I mingled and I partied in the Hollywood scene but somehow didn't feel how I expected I would at the end of the day.' The experience of returning home to support her mother helped her realise that there was something more to life than the whirlwind of her current life. She wrote, 'During my 2 weeks that I spent at home by her side, she made me realize that life is so precious and not to work it away doing something that is unfulfilling. I think it was truly that point that made me realize that I needed to be true to myself and what I wanted to do. I feel like I am finally where I am supposed to be *como si por fin he encontrado mi verdadera vocacion* [as if I have finally found my true vocation].'

Meet Nina: Nina, after 11 years as a successful payroll and benefits administrator, decided to enter the teaching profession because she 'felt dissatisfied inside'. Her memorable teachers include a high school Civics teacher who treated all students as adults, was very respectful, and encouraged his students to express their personal opinions in a safe and caring environment. Her second year Spanish teacher thought so highly of her Spanish abilities that Nina became a Teaching Assistant for the second year class once she had started the third year of Spanish. Nina wrote, 'She always encouraged me to strive for excellence.' Nina's favourite movie depicting the life of a teacher is 'Stand and Deliver' where Jaime Escalante shows how totally dedicated and committed he is to his students. Nina has had to overcome financial difficulties and not having valuable time for friends and family in order to become a teacher. The energy of the kids keeps her motivated, even though they sometimes are a challenge.

Results

Three generative themes emerged from the narratives of the interviewees who were becoming foreign language teachers. For each theme, excerpts are presented to illustrate the theme.

Theme 1

Foreign language student teachers were able to differentiate the Four Fs approach derided by multicultural educators from the Five Cs approach recommended by the World Language Council of 1996.

Bridget writes:

'There will always be discrepancies between theory and reality. However, I find it very interesting as a student teacher to see the differences between theory and reality in education. During this year of pedagogical theory in foreign language teaching, we have emphasized the five "C's" of foreign language teaching: communication, culture, comparisons, connections, and communities. In theory this would be the best way to teach a foreign language because it emphasizes all aspects of language. Unfortunately, what I have discovered in the real world of teaching is that foreign language teaching is based on whatever textbook has been adopted by that particular school district.

Due to this emphasis on the use of textbooks in classrooms, depending on what textbook your district has chosen, you will find it either easy or difficult to incorporate the five C's. During my student teaching experiences I have had the opportunity to use two different textbooks, *Acción* and *Ven Conmigo*. While I do not have the *Acción* textbook currently, I recall that culture was not emphasized at all. Everything we did was based on learning grammar. If I remember correctly, there was [*sic*] only a few pages per chapter dedicated to culture.

Currently I am using the *Ven Conmigo* series. This book definitely incorporates culture more so than the other book, but it focuses more on communication than culture. Each chapter contains *"Notas Culturales"* which are three to four sentences about different cultural aspects depending on what grammar/vocabulary is being studied. For example, in the chapter concerning food, there are "notas" regarding the different eating schedules in Spanish speaking countries. The chapters also contain *"Panoramas Culturales"* which are quotes from native speakers regarding whatever grammar/vocabulary is being studied.'

Laura explains her critique of the textbook

'A lot of what I have seen in *Pasos y Puentes* is a very narrow view of how things operate in Spain. Also the texts are somewhat outdated. There are some interesting aspects from the Spanish culture presented but most of it is extremely stereotypical. In my text, they want us just to present the small reading and answer a few target questions. Nothing too exciting to draw the students in and make them want to know more. Pretty dry reading!!!'

Theme 2

Textbooks dictated the type of teaching activities that student teachers were able to use in the classrooms.

Bridget writes

'The book contains *"Encuentros Culturales"* which are pages dedicated to going into more details regarding culture and that particular chapter. For example, in the chapter on food, the *Encuentro Culturale* is about the different foods that the Spaniards brought back from the new world, so that students realize that certain items are native to certain parts of the world. In a twenty-seven-page chapter, there are approximately three pages worth of culture. I feel that this does not adequately represent culture, especially if culture is supposed to be one fifth of what we teach. If this is true, then there should be about five full pages worth of "culture" in a twenty seven-page chapter. After having used two different text-books in my student teaching experience ,I have seen some of the differences in texts.

However, while textbooks play an important role, I have also found that teaching culture depends on the teacher's knowledge and desire to integrate it into the classroom and curriculum. It is my opinion that it shouldn't matter how much culture is represented in a given textbook, because it is up to the teacher to teach culture. In both of my experiences my cooperating teachers have seemed to leave culture by the wayside. They both seemed more focused on grammatical structures than culture. This is the exact opposite of the theory that we have learned during our credential course work. Thus I would say that there is defi-nitely a discrepancy between what is taught in theory to new teachers and what actually happens in the classroom. It doesn't matter if a textbook is full of culture if the teacher just ignores it.'

Nina writes:

'My textbook, called *En Espanol Uno*, addresses cultural aspects quite well in my opinion. I believe this is due in large part to the fact that it has been published more recently. It covers multiple facets of culture, not just food, fashion and festi-vals. Included are such varied topics as advertisements, animals, art, architec-ture, avenues, monuments, birthdays, city life, climate, clothing, daily life, food, geography, greetings, handicrafts, Hispanic influence in the U.S., history, money, people and many, many more. It also highlights regional differences in language from country to country. The references are fairly accurate, of high quality and in some cases very authentic. It would be even better if the book made comparisons between how you say something in one country vs. how you say the same thing somewhere else. In this respect the language connection appears to be a bit flat, one dimensional and less interesting. This, however, is the only negative thing I can really say about my textbook. It was actually of tremen-dous assistance to me in giving us an abundance of ideas for creating our unit on Ecuador.'

Theme 3

Student teachers saw that the textbook could be used as a basis for critical anal-yses, thematic instruction, and bringing in artifacts and other enriching aspects of culture.

Laura's voice:

'Well, I am teaching from *Pasos y Puentes* and the cultural aspects from this book are not reflective of what I have learned in my program and of the latino culture present in California and the United States. They are very European (all from Spain) and very dry. Culture, as I like to teach it and how I learned to teach it through my methods classes and [bicultural] courses, needs to be real and dynamic and should be presented in a relevant way. There is no right or wrong way to look at culture and nothing is set in stone. I like to bring in authentic sources, literature (children's books typical of the culture of choice) so that students have a more broad view of what it is like to be part of this other culture.'

Discussion

Why are these three themes from these three foreign language student teachers important for foreign language professors? First, the credibility of the case study approach is strengthened to the extent that the reader's experiences resonate with the experiences of Bridget, Laura and Nina. Second, the results of the interviews indicate that language teachers even at the student teacher level can tie in the teaching of culture using the Five Cs approach even when their textbooks might be actually presenting the Four Fs. Bridget's words reflect the dichotomy faced by many foreign language student teachers as they entered the field of education. On the one hand they are eager to apply the principles of critical pedagogy they had learned in their methods classes, but on the other hand they find themselves tied to a specific approach as presented by a given textbook. Bridget continues by reflecting on what she has faced in the classroom by giving a brief summary of the textbooks she used. It is evident that Bridget's reflections on the *Encuentros Culturales* section of the textbook point to the lack of incorporation of authentic culture and also the discrepancy between what the Foreign Language Standards indicate and what the textbook shows. Finally Bridget's words on how it is the teacher, and not the textbook, that should guide the teaching of culture show the importance of incorporating multicultural education and critical pedagogy in a teacher's preparation programme are echoed by Laura and Nina who describe actions that show foreign language teachers can build authentic classroom experiences from the sometimes 'dry' textbooks at their disposal. Finally, the veteran teacher's influence on the student teacher is evident as Bridget described her experiences with two cooperating teachers who were trained *before* the emphasis on communication and culture was a part of foreign language teaching.

Laura's words exemplify one of the main problems in the teaching of culture in the foreign language classroom. She points to the textbook's emphasis on the culture of Spain rather than the culture of all other Spanish-speaking countries, regardless of the fact that most of the foreign language students in the United States are closer to Mexico and Central America than Spain. Thus, the cultural base of the teacher can often influence (unconsciously) the perceptions and subsequent presentation of the cultural norms of the other culture.

What can foreign language professors do to prepare their candidates to develop and deliver well-articulated, integrated lessons designed to address the complex nature of culture instead of trivialising it? Professors can assist their teacher candidates to recognise and value the struggles involved in language acquisition and understanding cultures by tapping into the power of critical pedagogy principles. They can be encouraged by the emerging literature on critical pedagogy that suggests ways to tap into the struggle for self-awareness (*conscientization*) (Florez, 1998; Kluth *et al.*, 2002; Seufert, 1999).

For example, Seufert (1999) lists several methods that have a solid research base for improving language proficiency in speaking and using the language: 'Freirean and participatory approaches start with real issues in the learners' lives and develop the curriculum and language skills to address those issues, such as advocating for children, speaking up on the job, or dealing with legal problems.' Diaz-Greenberg (2003) provides a well-articulated example of applying a Freirean approach to the foreign language classroom. Kluth *et al.* (2002) described two participatory methods many educators use to increase awareness of social justice issues and at the same time address the more traditional achievement of course objectives and standards: *Dialogue Teaching* and *Critical Literacy* as explained below.

In *Dialogue Teaching*, students themselves help to generate the curriculum, designing their own instructional methods, and reporting their progress within a framework of consciousness raising group dynamics. In *Critical Literacy*, students become self-advocates, for example by watching videos or films of people from other cultures whose life-situations may be similar to their own. They can write an autobiography that is subjected to a critique of the language they use to describe themselves and their situations, comparing and contrasting their own perhaps culturally unique problem solving, life affirming ways of dealing with difficulties and challenges. Using methods such as these, the foreign language professor tones down the more traditionally didactic student-teacher interactions, rejects the often one-way hierarchical model of knower-to-learner, and sees students as people, as experts in their own lives and experiences.

Another promising classroom practice for professors to consider involves a paradigmatic shift on the part of the instructor. Instead of viewing the foreign language learner as deficient in proficiency, the teacher's interactions change towards deeper respect when viewing the learner as an emerging speaker and reader in the new language. As an example, Pruyn (1999: 190) uncovered differential patterns in

> the discursive classroom interactions of students and their teachers in two classroom settings in a predominantly Latina/o inner city school in Los Angeles. The pre-K through 5th grade school, comprised of 97% Latina/o and Spanish was the predominant language, with political and/or economic refugees from El Salvador and Guatemala. There were approximately 1900 students and 80 teachers who worked on a year-round schedule with a well staffed and administratively supported bilingual education program. The first group of students consisted of a teacher-formed and labeled 'remedial' Spanish reading group in a bilingual second-grade classroom. The teacher presided over the classroom where the hegemonic pedagogical structure *maintained* her learners as 'remedial.

In contrast, the second group of students were children from the same school who were placed in a Spanish reading enrichment programme. Several members of the second-grade 'low' reading group described previously also participated in this programme, as did other students who were labelled as 'reading below grade level'. The teacher in the second context was guided by a liberal (not radical) notion of education. Verbatim discourses between the teachers and the children show the differences between the two teachers: Susana 'the pedagogue proper' role and Pedro's 'situational literacy' role. Pruyn shows how Pedro's teaching techniques yielded a qualitatively different outcome.

Pedro's students were learning to *become* successful readers by *practicing* being successful readers, as opposed to learning to be 'remedial' and 'low' readers by practicing being 'remedial' and 'low' readers. These bilingual students gained competence in a set of skills that served to define and produce them as competent and capable.

Perhaps professors of foreign language can be enheartened to make a similar shift to focus on their college students' emerging proficiency instead of their deficiencies.

Freire (1998: 17) stated, 'There is no *teaching* without *learning*, and by that I mean more than that the act of teaching demands the existence of those who teach and those who learn'. Freire (1998: 18) explicated the professional responsibility of teachers (and, by extension, foreign language professors) to critically analyse their 'well lived and apprehended' teaching experiences. Freire's position is that literacy involves reading the world in such a way that one can read the word, and that by engaging in reading the wor(l)d, one can emerge with a different, more liberating, view of the world. By naming the world (he says, codifying the world) we have the possibility of changing our experience of the world we live in. People learning a new language similarly have the opportunity to read the world in a new way, through the words of the new language, and thus potentially transform their personal experience of the world.

Diaz-Greenberg (2003) applied the principles of critical pedagogy in a foreign language classroom (Spanish) with high school students (predominantly English speakers). She used a dialogic retrospection – a powerful teaching/learning procedure. Diaz-Greenberg received permission to conduct an action research project with her high school students: 18 Latinos (12 girls, 6 boys) in grades 10–12 (15 to 18 years old) who were all members of the Spanish-for-Spanish speakers programme advanced placement language class. Nine were bilingual students who came from Latin American and Caribbean nations and had been in the US for only a couple of years; nine were born and raised in the US. Most had maintained their Spanish language through parental contact. A note about their high school: the Latino population of the school had increased from 30 in 1981 to 211 in 1991, but there was only 1 male Latino teacher, 3 females, 1 female office clerk and 1 female cafeteria worker (and a parent volunteer for the Media Centre). No administrators could speak Spanish and there were no bilingual guidance counsellors.

The students formulated interview questions with a small group which selected the most representative questions and presented them to the whole class. The entire class then discussed the questions and voted on which ones they would incorporate in their interviews with a student partner. Diaz-Greenberg then analysed the resulting narratives written by the students for themes by using an open-ended, inductive approach. The students' comments were clustered around four central issues which provided 'an insight into their perceptions of their own realities and illuminate areas that students consider must be incorporated as part of the learning process' (Diaz-Greenberg, 1995: 79).

At the heart of a critical pedagogy approach, there is a subtle but important shift of attention to the student and the student's culture. Goldstein demonstrated that young Spanish/English second language learners with disabilities could effectively become collaborators with her in designing their curriculum. She concluded,

> as students and teachers begin to recognize students as decision makers in their own learning, lessons and activities will emerge from the dialogue. These lessons will be meaningful, powerful, and transformative for both the students and their teacher, because they will come from the willingness and commitment of both parties to struggle through the difficult issues our students face every day. (1995: 473)

The examination of foreign-language student teachers' reflections revealed how students' perceptions and voices may be used as a springboard to explore the realities existent within the school system. These student teachers promoted different approaches to and different understandings of the substance of educational change, in spite of the textbooks they used and the differing approaches of their mentor teachers.

Similarly, foreign language professors might discover new dimensions of competency in their students when they use instructional activities such as dialogue teaching, critical literacy, dialogic retrospection interview process, and a focus on emerging proficiency (rather than on deficiencies). These methods can help foreign language professors bring the culture alive, in the fashion of the Five Cs, and thus provide important models for future language teachers to use with their K-12 pupils.

Conclusions

The authors' experiences with their interviewees ring true when combined with emerging literature from other sources. Gabel (2001: 31), writing about the discrepancies experienced by student teachers with disabilities, commented,

> Reflective practice and the value of reflexivity between personal experience and pedagogy are common research themes today. However, teacher candidates often report a lack of encouragement to be reflective of their experiences ... and the ways those experiences can inform their pedagogy.

However, we believe that foreign-language professors can establish a climate of dialogue and dialectic within their university classrooms. When this happens, areas of silence can be identified and explored so as to advance the participation of all voices. We believe that foreign language professors can positively meet the challenge of preparing their graduates to teach a diverse population of immigrants, children of families displaced by war, children from ethnically and linguistically diverse backgrounds. When professors become liberatory educators on behalf of people from ethnically and culturally diverse populations as well as people who speak a multitude of different languages, the advantages and benefits of education can be more equally distributed to all the people.

Correspondence

Any correspondence should be directed to Dr Rosario Diaz-Greenberg, California State University San Marcos, San Marcos, CA 95001, USA (rdiaz_greenberg@hotmail.com).

References

ACTFL (American Council on Teaching of Foreign Languages) (2002) *Program Standards for the Preparation of Foreign Language Teachers.* On WWW at http://www.actfl.org/public/articles/ncate2002.pdf.

Axelrod, J., and Bigelow, D. (1962) *Resources for Language and Area Studies; A Report on an Inventory of the Language and Area Centers Supported by the National Defense Education Act of 1958.* ASIN: B00005XST3.

Banks, J. (2002) *Cultural Diversity and Education: Foundations, Curriculum, and Teaching* (4th edn). New York: John Wiley and Sons.

Diaz-Greenberg, R. (1995) The emergence of voice in Latino High School students. Unpublishe PhD thesis, University of San Francisco.

Diaz-Greenberg, R. (2003) *The Emergence of Voice in Latino High School Students.* New York: Peter Lang.

Diaz-Greenberg, R., Thousand, J., Cardelle-Elawar, M. and Nevin, A. (2000) What teachers need to know about the struggle for self-determination (conscientization) and self-regulation: Adults with disabilities speak about their education experiences. *Teaching and Teacher Education,* 837–847.

Dutcher (1996) *Overview of Foreign Language Education in the United States.* Washington DC: Center for Applied Linguistics, NCBE Resource Collection Series No. 6.

Florez, M.C. (1998) *ERIC Q&A.* Washington, DC: National Center for ESL Literacy Education. (EDRS No. ED 427 552).

Freire, P. (1970) *Pedagogy of the Oppressed.* New York: Seabury.

Freire, P. (1998) First Letter: Reading the World/Reading the Word. In *Teachers as Cultural Workers: Letters to Those who Dare to Teach.* Boulder, CO: Westview Press.

Gabel, S. (2001) 'I wash my face in dirty water.' Narratives of disability and pedagogy. *Journal of Teacher Education* 52 (1), 31–47.

Goldstein, B. (1995) Critical pedagogy in a bilingual special education classroom. *Journal of Learning Disabilities* 28 (8), 463–475.

Goodlad, J. (1984) *A Place Called School.* New York: McGraw-Hill.

Heaney, T. (1995) Issues in Freierean pedagogy. Thresholds in Education. University of Chicago. On WWW at: http://www.nl.edu/ace/index.html.

Kluth, P., Nevin, A., Thousand, J. and Diaz-Greenberg, R. (2002) Teaching for liberation: Promising practices from critical pedagogy and inclusive education to invent creative and collaborative cultures. In J. Thousand, R. Villa and A. Nevin (eds) *Creativity and Collaborative Learning: A Practical Guide for Empowering Students, Teachers, and Families in an Inclusive, Multicultural, and Pluralistic Society* (2nd edn) (pp. 71–84). Baltimore, MD: Paul H. Brookes.

Lange, D.L. (1999) Planning for and using the new national culture standards. In *Foreign Language Standards: Linking Research Theories, and Practices.* Chicago, IL: National Textbook Company in conjunction with the American Council on the Teaching of Foreign Languages.

Maturana, H. and Varela, F. (1992) *The Tree of Knowledge.* Boston, MA: Shambhala Publications.

Nieto, S. (1994) Lessons from students on creating a chance to dream. *Harvard Educational Review* 64 (4).

Phillips, J. and Draper, J. (1999) *The Five Cs: Standards for Foreign Language Learning.* New York: Heinle.

Pruyn, M. (1999)The power of classroom hegemony: An examination of the impact of formal and postformal teacher thinking in an inner-city latina/o school. In J. Kincheloe, S. Steinberg and L. Villaverde (eds) *Rethinking Intelligence: Confronting Psychological Assumptions about Teaching and Learning* (pp. 189–216). New York: Routledge.

Pufahl, Rhodes and Christian (2000) *Foreign Language Teaching: What the United States Can Learn From Other Countries.* Report prepared for the US Dept of Education's Comparative Information on Improving Education Practice (ERIC). On WWW at: http://www.cal.org/ericcll/countries.html.

Regional refugee ceilings and admissions to the United States (1998) Refugee Reports, 19

(12). In P. Seufert *Q & A Refugees as English Language Learners: Issues and Concerns*. On WWW at: http://www.cal.org./ncle/DIGETS/Refugee.htm.

Seufert, P. (1999) *Q & A Refugees as English Language Learners: Issues and Concerns*. ERIC. On WWW at: http://www.cal.org./ncle/DIGETS/Refugee.htm.

Silberman, C.E. (1970) *Crisis in the Classroom: The Remaking of American Education*. New York: Vintage.

Sirotnik, K. (1981) *What You See is What You Get: A Summary of Observations in over 1000 Elementary & Secondary Classrooms. A Study of Schooling in the United States* (Technical Report No. 29). University of California at Los Angeles, Graduate School of Education.

Sizer, T. (1997) *Horace's Compromise: The Dilemma of the American High School*. Boston, MA: Houghton Mifflin.

Sleeter, C. and Grant, C. (2002) *Making Choices for Multicultural Education: Five Approaches to Race, Class, and Gender*. New York: John Wiley and Sons.

Thousand, J., Diaz-Greenberg, R., Nevin, A., Cardelle-Elawar, M., Beckett, E. C. and Reese, R. (1999) Perspectives on a Freirean critical pedagogy approach to inclusion. *Remedial and Special Education*, 5–8.

Seidman, I.E. (1991) *Interviewing as Qualitative Research: A Guide for Researchers in Education and the Social Sciences*. New York: Teachers College Press.

Wolcott, H.F. (1990) *Writing up Qualitative Research*. Newbury Park, CA: Sage.

Villa, R. and Thousand, J. (1995) *Creating Inclusive Schools*. Alexandria, VA: Association for Supervision and Curriculum Development.